JERUSALEM OR A

Sermons and Adaresses

❧

PETER R. WATKINS

Jill

love from

Peter

October
2005

SWANMORE BOOKS

Published by Swanmore Books
7 Crofton Way
Swanmore
Southampton SO32 2RF

ISBN 0 954 1566 1 7

Front cover: The pulpit in the church of St Peter, Bishop's Waltham
which was presented to the Rector, Dr Robert Ward by Lancelot Andrewes,
Bishop of Winchester in 1626.

Cover illustrations reproduced by kind permission of
the Rector the Revd. Andy Davis.

Designed, typeset and produced by
John Saunders Design & Production, Abingdon OX13 5HU
Printed in Great Britain by Biddles Ltd
www.biddles.co.uk

Contents

Contents

Preface

I have never felt called to the ordained ministry. I have however from an early age felt called to preach though I have to admit that it may be related to the passion to communicate which led me as my full-time vocation into the teaching profession. I became a Methodist local preacher while I was still in the Sixth form at school. When, in my mid-40s, I joined the Church of England I soon became a Reader.

I used to believe that sermons were essentially spoken and should be delivered only in the context of worship. A book of sermons was a contradiction in terms. I am no longer so sure. Sermons which assume familiarity with the Bible are no longer as accessible as they once were. The opportunity to return to them later with an open Bible may be one appreciated by many churchgoers.

My title is taken from a sermon on Paul's address to the Athenians recorded in the Acts of the Apostles chapter 17. It represents my conviction that we must try to connect with the varied religious experiences of the great majority of people who do not attend church.

Sermons date almost as quickly as yesterday's newspaper. I have updated some references but not all. Sermons are made to be spoken and heard not written and read. I have made some changes to accommodate the written word but I hope the resonances of the spoken word remain. I have added Biblical references which would have been intrusive in preaching.

These sermons and addresses are collected and published because some of those who heard them have asked for them in more permanent form.

I am grateful to Jill and Graham who cast their eyes over my first draft and found errors which had escaped my notice and to Kate who again contributated her computing skills.

September 2005   Peter Watkins

Dedicated to the memory of
The Reverend Whitfield Foy
Minister of Wesley Church , Cambridge 1952–1955 & 1967–1971
and to the congregations of St.Peter's, Bishop's Waltham and
the Blessed Mary, Upham
where most of these sermons were preached.

On Preaching

[Preaching] is the manifestation of the Incarnate Word, from the Written Word by the spoken word. Bernard Lord Manning 1892-1941, Senior Tutor of Jesus College, Cambridge and Congregational layman.[1]

Methodist local preacher and Anglican reader

On a July evening over 50 years ago I went with another local preacher to the Methodist chapel in the Warwickshire village of Nether Whitacre and preached my first sermon. The text, *Choose you this day whom ye will serve ...but as for me and my house we will serve the Lord.* (Joshua 24.15 AV) was singularly inappropriate since the elderly country folk who formed the bulk of the congregation had, many years before, decided that they would serve the Lord. I chose as the first hymn, number one in the then Methodist Hymn Book, *O for a thousand tongues to sing my great Redeemer's praise;* the congregation fell just 972 below the hymn's aspiration.

I had become what was called a local preacher 'on note', authorised to assist another local preacher in the conduct of worship. Six months later I became a local preacher 'on trial' permitted to take services on my own. I passed written examinations on the Old and New Testaments and on Christian doctrine, including John Wesley's *Notes on the New Testament* and his *Forty Four Sermons,* was examined orally by the local preachers' meeting, gave an account of 'my present Christian experience and call to preach', and, now at university, became at the tender age of 19, a 'fully accredited' local preacher.

When I recall my early sermons I blush at the sheer presumption of a schoolboy preaching to people whose experience of life and faith was so much longer and more profound than anything he could offer. Having said that I am glad that I learnt to preach early, because preaching is rather like learning to drive a car – the earlier you start the better. I am also grateful for the encouragement and forbearance of members of the congregations who heard my early sermons.

In my mid-forties I became a member of the Church of England and within a year or so a Reader, 'admitted and licensed' at Evensong in Chichester Cathedral by the Bishop of Chichester. It was in some ways a very different experience. I now conducted services of Morning and

Evening Prayer according to the *Book of Common Prayer*, administered the chalice at Holy Communion and sometimes preached, all in the church which I attended rather than in the churches of a Methodist Circuit. I was expected to base sermons on the lectionary. I no longer planned the services which I conducted, choosing hymns and lessons to fit my sermon. In the Methodist Church hymns were integral to the service and their choice the prerogative of the preacher; in the Church of England they were incidental to the service and usually chosen by the organist.

Preaching as a lay activity

In reflecting on preaching I do so therefore from the point of view of both a Methodist local preacher and an Anglican Reader. But I have also heard countless sermons and have always been fascinated by the craft of preaching. I heard the great London Methodist trio of the 1950s: W.E.Sangster at the Central Hall, Westminster, Leslie Weatherhead at the City Temple, and Donald Soper at Kingsway Hall, all often preaching to packed congregations. I also listened to the intensely Biblical preaching of John Stott at All Souls', Langham Place and Martyn Lloyd Jones at Westminster Chapel.

But it was preaching by laymen and women which was distinctive of Methodism. Without lay preachers Methodism would never have expanded as it did in the nineteenth century. The Church of England has traditionally regarded preaching as a clerical activity. There were no Readers in the Church of England until 1866 and even then their role was strictly regulated in case they should appear to usurp clerical functions. Only since 1969 have women been admitted as Readers. In recent years there has been a much greater acceptance of laity in Anglican pulpits, in part at least because of the decline in the number of clergy and the development of multi-parish benefices.

I believe it is important for lay people to preach. Professor Dennis Nineham, in his book *The Use and Abuse of the Bible*, wrote 'The time is past when sermons from lay members of the church could be regarded as an optional extra. They are now vital for a faith with potentiality for survival. So many aspects of contemporary culture are bound to be a closed book to the clergy and other theologians that it is vital for lay Christians who do know about contemporary culture to play a much larger part in theological debate than they have ever done before'. [2] There seems to me much work to be done on how we ensure that the inter-face between faith and working life is included in our sermons. Laity ought to bring to preaching a dimension which clergy cannot.

Preaching then and now

Preaching as a means of communicating the faith has greatly diminished in all denominations since the 1960s in part because of the decline of church attendance, but also because of the rise of competition from radio and television. Professor Adrian Hastings dated the decline to the mid-1950s when 'people suddenly ceased to think it worthwhile listening to a special preacher'. [3] We now live in the world of the sound bite, the simulation, the workshop, the short interview and the question and answer session. It is not only in the church that formal communication is much less acceptable. In school, teaching and learning styles are less formal; we no longer stand in front of the class and talk while the pupils listen; learning must be active. Politicians no longer address great rallies. They engage in the cut and thrust of doorstep debate. We have lost our faith in preaching and our readiness to listen. It is no longer possible for a busy minister of any denomination to spend hours each week in preparing Sunday sermons.

The style of preaching has changed accordingly. Sermons are shorter. Few Anglican congregations expect more than 15 minutes and often the sermon is shorter still. It was John Ruskin, the nineteenth century artist, poet and social reformer who described preaching as 'Thirty minutes in which to wake the dead', for today's preacher it is all too often 'Fifteen minutes in which to keep the living awake'. The sermons of 50 years ago invariably began with a Biblical text whether or not the sermon which followed was a faithful exposition of it. The style was often oratorical, full of sonorous phrases and rhetorical devices, embellished by gesture and mannerism. Humour was rare and jokes unknown. Laughter, once next to blasphemy, is now close to godliness.

Methodist and Anglican preaching

There is still a difference between Methodist and Anglican preaching though the two have grown closer in recent years. Anglicans now take preaching more seriously and Methodists are more liturgically aware. Methodist sermons are generally better constructed. A Methodist service is as dependent on the sermon as an Anglican service is on the Eucharist. When I learnt to preach I was urged to study W.E.Sangster's *The Craft of Sermon Construction* and *The Craft of Sermon Illustration*. The typical Methodist sermon had an introduction, three main points and a conclusion, not a bad model provided it doesn't become too stereotyped. Methodists now use the lectionary much more than they did in my youth. We were not expected to preach from the lectionary except at major festivals. You could preach the same sermon several times at different churches. Sermons can improve with familiarity provided, in the words of Dr Sangster, you can 'glow' over them again. [4] As Colin Morris asserts: ' Any sermon in which a preacher has invested honest effort ought to be heard again. Beethoven didn't compose his sonatas to be played once'.[5]

Methodists prepare sermons, Anglicans write sermons. When I was a Methodist I never read a sermon, now I often do though I recall the church member who commented to a preacher,' If *you* can't remember your sermon, there's not much chance I shall'. The greatest compliment my father could pay to a Methodist preacher was to say 'And he hadn't got a note', though I suspect that some preachers were better at concealing their notes than others. There was however the expectation that the sermon was inspired by the Spirit, that the preparation had taken place in the study and that all that was needed in the pulpit was a few headings

What is a sermon?

The dictionary describes a sermon as 'a discourse delivered in church', but the colloquial use of the word is more discouraging. '*Sermon*: a dressing down, harangue, a talking to', '*To preach*: to moralise in a tedious manner'. What then is a sermon? It is a curious hybrid. Let me set out five characteristics which in my view a sermon should possess in some degree.

Content A sermon must have content and will usually take its origin from the Bible. Clergy and Readers spend much time in the course of their training reading books on the Bible, writing essays and discussing its relevance to contemporary issues. But of course no sermon should be a lecture. The content has to be digested, internalised and applied to the needs of the congregation. The congregation is entitled to expect the preacher whether clerical or lay to take account of the findings of Biblical scholarship. They should become aware for example that Moses did not write the first five books of the Bible, that not all of Isaiah was written at the same time, that Jesus did not say all the things attributed to him in the gospels and that John's gospel is a different sort of book from the other three.

You sometimes hear people say ' He (or she) was above my head this morning'. It is rarely true. Almost any sermon topic can be explained in terms which any member of the congregation can understand. If the sermon is incomprehensible the fault is that of the preacher not the congregation. 'Don't talk down to your congregation; it isn't there', wrote Dr Russell Maltby, a distinguished Methodist minister of the first half of the twentieth century in his *Twenty four precepts for preachers*. I am always glad when somebody says to me after I have preached, ' I didn't agree with what you said' – at least it shows they were listening. I'm even more pleased when they say ' I'd never thought of it like that before'.

Structure The content needs to be organised. On sermon construction Dr Maltby wrote 'The well is deep and you must have something to draw with but there is no need to make the congregation drink out of the bucket still less chew the rope'. Or to put the same point in a homely aphorism: 'I tells 'em what I'm going to tell 'em'; I tells' em, and I tells 'em I've told 'em'. The congregation needs to know where you are going and every now and again reminded where you've got to. The end of the sermon should be natural and expected not like an express train hitting the buffers or a car gradually running out of petrol. As for style, a sermon, like a political speech, needs controlled repetition. The preacher needs to say things more than once if they are to lodge in the minds of the congregation but using different words and phrases so that the repetition does not become monotonous.

Illustration There was a time when preacher and congregation would both appreciate erudite quotations from the plays of Shakespeare or the poetry of Robert Browning. Today illustrations are more down to earth. They are likely to be drawn from television soaps, from popular plays, films or newspapers. Their function is to provide a concrete image, a point of contact and a shared experience. It is often the illustrations which the congregation remembers long after the main thrust of the sermon has been forgotten. It is important therefore that what the illustration is meant to illustrate should be clear.

Sermons should be interesting. As Bernard Manning puts it, addressing ministers in training from the point of view of the man or woman in the pew: 'To interest your hearers is your first job. ... It does not matter how long you preach nor even how short, how eloquently, truly, orthodoxly, heretically, sincerely, how loudly or how inaudibly you preach, if people are bored you might as well be silent'.[6]

Application The sermon needs to relate to the lives we actually live. It will therefore have about it a touch of immediacy so that we can recall it when we are involved in a boardroom dispute, coping with a difficult class of pupils, engaged in a family argument or caught in a traffic jam. The preacher should bear this immediacy in mind in the content, the language in which the sermon is couched and in its presentation. You may remember or have heard a tape of *Beyond the fringe,* the satirical review of the early 1960s. It included a spoof sermon preached by Alan Bennett on the text (a genuine one) 'My brother Esau is an *hairy* man, but *I* am a smooth man.' (Genesis 27.11) It was a superb pastiche of all the worst errors which a preacher can commit – among them the clerical voice, spurious piety, vagueness, irrelevance, attempted ingratiation with the congregation – ' Is there bit in the corner of the sardine tin of your life? I know there is in mine'.

The ring of truth A sermon is not a personal testimony – it would be embarrassing if it were. It should however have about it the ring of truth, which comes from personal experience and genuine conviction. Don't preach your doubts we were told but equally don't pretend to certainties you don't feel. Lay people are often ashamed of doubts they think clergy don't have or would be shocked to learn that they have. I have sometimes said things from the pulpit and been thanked for being frank –'I've often thought that too'. In the introduction to his book of sermons *The True Wilderness*, Harry Williams, then Dean of Trinity College, Cambridge, now a Mirfield Father writes 'I resolved that I would not preach about any aspect of Christian belief unless it had become part of my own lifeblood.. I realised that the Christian truth I tried to proclaim would speak to those who listened only to the degree to which it was an expression of my own identity.'[7] It is an aspiration which I have certainly not achieved but it is a reminder of the importance of truth in preaching.

I have heard countless sermons in the course of my life but I can recall very few of them. I used to worry about that until I came across this illustration. A man whose wife had cooked him 3,650 meals in the previous ten years commented that he couldn't remember what any of them had consisted of. Beef, pork, chicken and lamb had figured prominently and so had carrots, potatoes and peas. How they had been cooked and served he hadn't any idea. He knew however that he had a balanced diet and was well-nourished, fit and active.

1. B.L.Manning *A layman in the ministry* Independent press 1942 p138
2. D.E.Nineham *The use and abuse of the Bible* 1977 p.246
3. Adrian Hastings *A history of English Christianity 1920–2000* p.465
4. W.E.Sangster *The craft of sermon construction* Epworth press 1949 p.194
5. Colin Morris *Raising the dead* Fount 1996 p.63
6. B.L Manning *op cit* p.143
7. Harry Williams *The True Wilderness* Constable 1965 p.8

THE CHURCH YEAR

Advent

Keep awake. Matthew 24.42
*You know what time it is; it is the moment for you to wake out
of sleep.* Romans 13.11

Sir Edwyn Hoskyns, a great New Testament scholar of the 1920s and 30s,
told how in his youth he went to a service in a remote Lakeland village. The
church was full and there was an atmosphere of pent-up excitement. The
reason for the crowd and the excitement soon became clear: the Vicar had
let it be known that he would reveal the date of the end of the world and
what his parishioners should do to prepare for it.

Today such announcements are usually made by door-to-door evangelists
rather than Anglican Vicars. We smile indulgently or slam the door impa-
tiently according to our temperament. We know that the end of the world is
not likely to be imminent and so we can safely ignore the warnings.

Apocalyptic literature

The difficulty for preachers on Advent Sunday is that they are confronted
with gospel readings which do suggest that the end is near even if the date is
not known. Today we read a passage from Matthew 24, but there are similar
readings in Mark 13 and Luke 21. They belong to a type of literature called
apocalyptic, which we associate chiefly with the book of Daniel in the Old
Testament and the book of Revelation in the New Testament. Apocalyptic
means unveiling, it is a body of literature produced by the Jews between
about 250 BC and 200 AD, which was taken up and used by Christians. The
future course of events they believed could be discerned through visions or
disclosed through dreams, which tell us about the crises which will accom-
pany the end of history when the forces of evil will be destroyed and the
world will be restored as God intended it to be.

Apocalyptic literature helped to sustain hope and perseverance among
people who faced opposition or persecution for their faith. The gospel
writers in the apocalyptic sections of their writings wanted to enable
Christians to face the future, whatever it might bring, with patience, perseverance and hope.

Most scholars would say that Jesus himself probably thought the end of
the world would take place soon and the early church had similar expecta-

tions. There is of course a huge gap between the thought world of the first century and the twenty first century and most Christians, at least in the west, no longer feel they are living in the last days; we do not expect the end of the world to take place in the way described in the apocalyptic parts of the New Testament. How then do we respond to the Advent readings in the gospels? They address two questions which people are still asking. First what is the meaning of human history? And second what is the Christian response to it? Let me speak briefly about each.

What is the meaning of human history?

A variety of answers has been given over the years to the meaning of human history

To the *Greeks* history was a huge circle, a pattern of death and decay followed by rebirth and renewal. It was exemplified in the myth of the phoenix – the bird that died in the flames and then rose from the embers. History was like the cycle of nature – spring, summer, autumn and winter. One of the hymns we sing at Christmas contains a verse, which encapsulates the Greek view of history: *It came upon the midnight clear.*

> For lo! the days are hastening on,
> By prophet bards foretold,
> When with the ever-circling years
> Comes round the age of gold.
> When peace shall over all the earth
> Its ancient splendours fling,
> And the whole world give back the song
> Which now the angels sing.

To the *Victorians* history was a line pointing upwards, the story of human progress. God's kingdom was coming as human beings got better and better, and society steadily improved. *And I doubt not through the ages one increasing purpose runs,* wrote Tennyson in 1842 in his poem *Locksley Hall.* That notion is to be found in many Victorian hymns most of which have now disappeared from our hymn-books, for example John Addington Symonds: *These things shall be.*

> Nation with nation, land with land,
> Unarmed shall live as comrades free;
> In every heart and brain shall throb,
> The pulse of one fraternity.

That view of history, as the story of inevitable progress, was shattered for ever by the experience of the First World War though its dying flicker can be discerned in the slogan, which looked back on the recently ended conflict describing it as : 'The war to end all wars'.

To *Marxists* history was a struggle between social classes which would end in worldwide proletarian revolution – a vision which inspired generations of communists.

Then there is the *secular humanist* view of history – a meaningless procession of events, just one thing after another.

But the Christian view of history is none of these – the Greek, the Victorian, the Marxist and the humanist are all equally fallacious. For us the whole meaning of history is to be found in events which took place 2000 years ago. It is the birth, death and Resurrection of Jesus which lays bare once and for all the meaning of human history. All subsequent and all previous history is seen and judged by it. The events which we celebrate through the church year do not recede as the years go by; we are as close to the incarnation now as we ever were. History is a circle but at the centre of the circle is the event round which all else revolves. A Christian judgement on history sees all events as instruments of God's judgement in love and mercy. It is this which helps us to interpret those difficult apocalyptic passages in the gospels.

The urgency of our response

Let me turn second to the response which is required of us and which is a feature of the readings from Romans and from Matthew's gospel. The readings and the hymns we sing in Advent have as their insistent refrain the need to be prepared, to be ready for whatever may happen. In the gospel reading this morning Matthew provides two vivid pictures of how the followers of Jesus are to prepare.

The first is a cartoon of the Old Testament story of Noah. Noah's friends – men and women alike – are going about their daily work, business as usual, while he and his family are building a boat. No doubt they thought he was crazy until it started to rain and didn't stop and Noah and his family got into the Ark while the flood overwhelmed the onlookers. 'Be like Noah', says Jesus, 'be prepared even if people do laugh at you'.

The second picture is of a householder who went to bed and slept soundly only to discover in the morning that his house had been broken into and the thieves had got the television, the video and the computer. And the moral – Keep awake, be alert.

That's the message of Advent. It is conveyed in the parable of the Wise and Foolish Virgins in the next chapter of Matthew on which what I regard as the greatest Advent hymn is based: *Sleepers Wake* sung to that wonderful Bach Chorale *Wachet Auf*.

Responses – individual, church and world

The call to keep awake comes to us as individuals, as members of the church and as citizens of God's world. Let me say a word about each.

There is urgency first of all about our daily lives as Christians. Don't delay in settling a quarrel or restoring a relationship – you never know when it may be too late. Don't put off contributing to Water Aid or to the pressing needs of the Third World – people are dying out there. Don't delay in witnessing to the call to racial harmony whenever you can – we live in a multi-racial world.

Second this is a word which we need to hear as a church. The Church of England produces almost endless excuses for delay – there is for example 'need for further study', 'for discernment' or opportunity for ' reception' of an idea or course of action. Conversations between the Church of England and the Methodist Church lasted from 1955 to 1969 – 14 years. When decision time came we drew back and decided to play for safety and a great opportunity was lost. Recently the Rochester report on women as bishops was published. It had taken four years to produce. We were told that if it were agreed that women could be bishops it could not happen before about 2010. I am reminded of that extra verse of Onward *Christian Soldiers* which you may not remember singing:

> Like a mighty tortoise
> Moves the church of God
> Brothers we are treading
> Where we've always trod.

Finally the Advent call to keep awake is addressed to us as citizens in God's world. A year or two ago the Bishop's Adviser on Ecology was invited to the Deanery Synod. He spoke to us about environmental issues with a good deal of vivid detail – about the destruction of the ozone layer that protects life on earth, about climate changes which result from greenhouse gases, about the worldwide loss of an area of forest the size of Britain every year. And he reminded us that as Christians *The earth is the Lord's* and we are his stewards. Wake up, he said – it's urgent. Don't shy away because the issues are complex and solutions painful. I am delighted that we have this year become an Eco congregation, one that takes seriously the Advent call urgently to hear God speaking to us about the care of His world long after we are dead. Our parish team recently gave a presentation to the Deanery Synod so perhaps we shall soon be the first Eco Deanery. Remember the slogan we were given: 'We don't own the earth, we borrow it from our grandchildren.'

Perhaps after all those Lakeland villagers were right. There ought to be an atmosphere of excitement and anticipation as we hear again the Advent message: *Keep awake. You know what time it is; it is the moment to wake out of sleep.*

ᴥ

Incarnation

Many deceivers have gone out into the world, those who do not confess Jesus Christ has come in the flesh. 2 John 7

The church year which provides the framework for our worship week by week is all about comings and goings. Jesus comes through the gateway of birth at Bethlehem and goes through the gateway of death in Jerusalem on Good Friday. He comes through Resurrection on Easter Day and according to the Acts of the Apostles ascends to the Father 40 days later. He comes a third time through the Holy Spirit at Pentecost to be with us for ever.

Today we come to the end of the events which constitute that first coming, the one which we call the Incarnation. We prepared for it in Advent, and now we celebrate it at with shepherds and angels at Christmas. The question I want to ask today is how do we recognise his coming to us at the beginning of the twenty first century.

How does God come to us through Jesus?

He comes to us first of all through prayer and worship. We come to church on Sundays and on special occasions to encounter God, through hymns and prayers, through Bible readings and sermon and above all through the Eucharist. At Christmas we meet him through the beauty of a decorated church, through the resonances of familiar words in readings and carols, through Carol service and Crib service and through Holy Communion at midnight on Christmas Eve.

Second we experience his coming through our emotions. There are men and women in Christian ministry as well as lay people who can give a date when they were challenged and heard God speak to them unmistakably and

17

whose lives were transformed forever as a result. Our emotions may be stirred to meet the Lord through the joy of human love, through the beauty of nature, through music and poetry, through the experience of depth and meaning to which these gave rise.

There are some thirdly who encounter God in the apparently miraculous. The Roman Catholic church in particular finds proof of God's working and Jesus' presence through the miraculous. In 1998 Monica Besra, a woman living in West Bengal was diagnosed with terminal stomach cancer. Against all the odds she recovered and attributed her restored health to the intervention of Mother Theresa. It was a further step towards the canonisation of Mother Theresa as a saint. Pope John Paul II attributed his recovery from the assassination attempt in 1981 to the intercession of the Blessed Virgin Mary. There are of course people right outside the Roman Catholic tradition who can describe miraculous intervention in their lives bringing healing and wholeness to them and to friends and relations.

And finally some people experience the presence of God through the otherwise inexplicable. When John Wesley was aged five in 1709 the roof of Epworth Rectory where he lived went on fire. It was made of thatch and the fire was fierce. Young John was rescued in the nick of time. Forever afterwards he was convinced that God had intervened and he had been saved for a purpose. He described himself as ' A brand plucked from the burning', the title which Roy Hattersley gave to his biography of Wesley.

More prosaic are the notices you sometimes get through the door advertising a meeting which will take place 'DV', God willing. The meeting will happen unless God stops it. Perhaps the central heating will break down, or the speaker suffer a sudden debilitating illness because the Lord does not wish the meeting to happen. Or there is the phrase beloved of lawyers, an Act of God, against which you cannot insure, a flood, earthquake, or other unforeseen disaster, which can only be attributed to the intervention of God.

You may have heard the phrase 'the God of the gaps'. It was coined by Professor Charles Coulson, Oxford professor and Methodist layman.[1] We have, he said, used God to fill the gaps where science can at the moment provide no explanation. The problem is that as scientific knowledge expands the gaps left for God contract and he is squeezed out of his universe.

A friend of mine served for a long time as Vicar in a tough parish in a northern city. As he got older he needed a less demanding parish. He sought God's guidance and shortly afterwards was offered the living of a village in the Yorkshire Dales. He had never heard of this village but in subsequent weeks he heard its name mentioned frequently by friends, in shops and in the bank. This must, he concluded, be God's way of telling him that this was where he should be, so he accepted the living.

We may expect to meet God then through worship, through our emotions, through the miraculous and through the apparently inexplicable and coincidental. And of course God does come to some people in those ways.

He comes in flesh

But he does not come exclusively in these ways. Jesus took our flesh – all of it. We must be sure that we do not relegate his coming to the fringes of life, we must not associate him with fragments of experience not the whole, we must be careful not to think of him as somebody who occasionally reminds us that he is there like a visitor from a foreign country. He is not 'the God of the gaps'.

Incarnation means that the Jesus who came in flesh once, goes on coming in flesh, in the whole of our human experience not just in part of it. He is known through scientific knowledge not through scientific gaps. The circumstances of his birth remind us how representative was his coming – born in temporary lodgings, a vulnerable baby, to a human mother, in an occupied country, ruled by a tyrant. Nothing more fully human can be imagined.

The text I have used this morning comes from the shortest book in the entire Bible the Second Letter of John. It contains a mere 13 verses, not more than a reasonable length paragraph. It was written probably in the first 20 years of the second century AD to people who said God was to be found in special revelations and extraordinary visions. The writer of the letter corrects them ' Many deceivers, he says, 'have gone out into the world, those who do not confess that Jesus Christ has come in the flesh... Be on your guard, so that you do not lose what we have worked for' (verses 7,8)

God comes through the whole of human experience

Jesus comes to us then through the whole of our human experience – in flesh once, in flesh now.

- *In worship* We speak sometimes of 'coming into the presence of God' as we enter the church, as though he were locked up in the building where we left him last Sunday. Meanwhile we trekked through the desert of our workaday existence until we reached the next oasis on Sunday. But in fact we meet God here on Sunday because we bring with us all the other meetings with him during the week. Our worship is not an escape from life but an endorsement, a summing up which gives coherence and significance to everything else.

- *Through emotion* Yes but also through mind, body and will, through work and leisure, meetings and relationships, colleagues and opponents.

- *Through the miraculous* But also through healing and wholeness mediated by doctors, nurses, social workers and psychiatrists. If Mother Theresa qualifies for sainthood it is because she devoted her life to care for those living in the slums of Calcutta not because she is thought by some to be the instrument of miraculous cures.

- *Through the inexplicable* But also through the normal meetings of everyday life. My friend moved from the inner city to the Yorkshire Dales because the country parish needed a priest with his gifts, he needed a less demanding parish and when he met the churchwardens they were convinced he was the right person. He moved as a result of ordinary processes through which God spoke.

  The God of creation speaks to us not through the gaps in our knowledge of science but through our expanding awareness of the universe in which he has placed us.

Religious experience is not a special category. It is ordinary experience interpreted differently because through it we meet Jesus Christ coming in the flesh. One final point. Coming in flesh means he comes in the whole of human experience, some of it tragic, as well as the joyful and the fulfilling. He comes through the experience of frustration, tension, and failure as well as success; through the experience of guilt, suffering and death as well as healing and wholeness; through the experience of being lost as well as found. Dr Frances Young, Professor of Theology at Birmingham University and a Methodist minister tells how it was the experience of being the mother of a profoundly handicapped child which led her to offer for the ministry.

The text from the second Letter of John strikes a negative note. The same message is put positively in a better-known text. *The word became flesh and dwelt among us.* John 1.14

1. C.A.Coulson *Science and Christian belief* Fontana 1958 pp.32,41

Epiphany

Matthew 2.1–12, Isaiah 60. 1-6, Ephesians 3.1-12

Just before Christmas my newspaper said 'Stop going crackers, wrapping presents and making mince pies and find out how you score in this quiz.' So I did.

Question 1 why do we put brandy over the Christmas pudding and light it? Pass. Question 2 why do we kiss under the mistletoe? Speak for yourself. Question 3 who made the first Christmas crib and when? I looked that one up – St Francis of Assisi in 1223. Never mind I thought, I'll do better on the Biblical questions. Question 1 how many Wise Men were there? Easy – three. Question 2 what sort of people were they. Kings. Question 3 what were their names? Caspar, Melchior and Balthazar. Question 4 what did they look like? One came from Africa and was black; one came from Europe and was white and one came from Asia and had yellow skin.

The wise men in later legends

Well of course all my answers were wrong or at least you cannot find the answers in the Bible. St Matthew's gospel, which tells the story of the Wise Men doesn't say how many there were, what their names were or what they looked like. He tells us that there were three *gifts* not three wise men. He tells that they were *magoi*, astrologers or wise men – no mention of kings. It is from references in Psalm 72 (verses 10–11) and Isaiah 60 (verse 3) that later commentators concluded that they were kings. As for their names they are not found until the sixth century when Caspar is described as a young, black, beardless man who brought myrrh as his gift to the infant king; Melchior as an old man, with a grey beard whose gift was gold and Balthazar a middle-aged man who brought frankincense. In the Middle Ages the wise men were venerated as saints. Their alleged relics were taken to Germany in 1162 and are to be found in Cologne Cathedral.

So Matthew's simple unadorned story has grown over the centuries and been embellished with legends. The story of the Wise Men has caught the imagination of artists and around it have grown some of our best-loved Christmas carols, for example *We three kings of orient are*, and *Three kings from Persian lands afar*. The story has inspired poets. You probably know T.S.Eliot's *Journey of the Magi* which begins 'A cold coming we had of it. /

Just the worst time of year for a journey', or W.H.Auden's *For the time being* which includes the lines 'To discover how to be human now/ is the reason we follow the star'. And of course countless sermons have been preached on the Wise Men commenting on the representative nature of the men and the symbolic significance of the gifts they brought.

The significance of the wise men

Why then did Matthew – and only Matthew – include the story of the Wise Men in his gospel? Matthew's gospel was probably written by a Jewish Christian who saw Jesus as the fulfilment of Old Testament prophecy. He frequently says, 'All this took place in order to fulfil what was spoken by the lord through the prophet saying…' but he also realised that many Jews did not accept this and so a mission to the Gentile world was now the task.

The Wise Men who come from the east are contrasted with Herod and the Jewish establishment. They represent the intellectual elite of the pagan world who are true worshippers and come to worship the infant king. They set out from the east, they commend themselves to God's guidance and they bring gifts. Herod on the contrary sees Jesus as a rival, tries to involve the Wise Men in his malicious intention to destroy him. He is to Matthew a symbol of unbelief and hardness of heart which characterises the religious leaders and the Jewish people. So the meaning of the story which Matthew tells is the replacement of the Jews by the Gentiles, the non-Jewish world, as the object of the coming of Jesus.

Isaiah 60 and Ephesians 3

Both the other readings this morning have a link with the theme of the Wise Men. The passage in Isaiah chapter 60 has camels and kings, gold and frank-incense. Here too the nations grasp the significance of events which the Jews miss. God's coming, says the writer, brings light not only to the Jews but to all nations.

In Ephesians chapter three the writer says that what he calls 'the mystery of Christ', which was once confined to the Jews has now been revealed to all. The Gentiles are 'fellow heirs, members of the same body, sharers in the promise'. Each phrase in the verse uses the same Greek prefix *syn* which means 'together' so you could translate the passage – heirs together, a body together, sharers together. The heart of the mystery says the writer is the unity of all people in the intention of God. That then is what the three readings are all about – the story of the Wise Men in Matthew, the reading from

Isaiah in the Old Testament and the New Testament passage from Ephesians.

The unity of all humanity

What then does the story of the Wise Men say to us in the twenty first century? We are I believe obliged to confront an uncomfortable truth. Matthew opens up the circle of salvation to all nations. But we can no longer confront the great world faiths as inadequate and their members as needing to become Christians. We are too aware of how much damage this has done over the centuries. Anti-Semitism – hostility to Jews, often virulent and murderous – has its origins in the New Testament. The belief that the Jews were responsible for the death of Christ has been used as an excuse to persecute them. In the reign of Edward I Jews were expelled from England and only readmited by Oliver Crowell 400 years later. In many European cities they were confined to a Jewish ghetto.

We see too in our world the monstrous evil released by Moslem fundamentalism. For us Jesus is the Way, the Truth and the Life, the way in which we find God. But for other faiths there are ways which to their followers have equal validity. It is this truth which we need to set alongside the uniqueness of Christ for us. Let me illustrate.

Nobody will ever forget seeing on television the fall of the Twin Towers of the World Trade Centre in New York on 11th September 2001, shown repeatedly in the following days, a day called ever since 9/11. I recall a service held two months later in Westminster Abbey to commemorate the British victims of 9/11. It was attended by the Queen and the Prime Minister amongst many others. In the huge congregation were representatives of all faiths and of course the service was televised. The most moving moment for me came at the end when representatives of all the world's great faiths and of all the main Christian communions, each dressed in their distinctive robes, gathered on the altar steps and pledged their faith community to seek justice, peace, reconciliation and the unity of all humanity. That I believe is the message of that moving passage in Ephesians for the twenty first century: heirs together, a body together, sharers together not only in the gospel, but in our God-given humanity.

Too often our vision of humanity has been exclusive, not inclusive, for all – as long as they are Christians, not Jews, Muslims, Buddhists, Hindus, people of any other faith or none. In the twenty first century it will not do – our vision has to be inclusive. Sadly it is division, hatred, strife and war, which make headlines. News items are rarely fashioned out of unity, love, and the achievement of peace. And even more sadly Christians are not blameless either. We still exalt what separates rather than what unites us. Our evangelism has led us sometimes to discount and look down on the insights of the other great world faiths. Let's keep our evangelism in future for those of no faith and let's celebrate the truths and cultures of the faiths now often represented in our own country. And if that's heresy, I'm content to be a heretic.

Colin Morris has a book called *Mankind my church*. (It was published in 1971. If he were writing it now I'm sure it would be entitled *Humankind my church*). In it he has a sermon with the same title based on Ephesians 3.18, *Consider what is the breadth and length and height and depth of the love of God*. He says this:

> I am more than a Methodist, more than a Protestant; yes more even than a Christian. I am first and foremost a member of the human race, and so to that must be my primary allegiance. ...If there is a boundary between faith and unfaith running somewhere through the community of men [and women] only God knows where it is. No mortal. has the right to draw such a line and so set [themselves] up as a judge over their fellow [human beings]. ... Jesus is a member of the [church] which embraces all [human] kind; no other [church] is big enough to hold him. He is the one who by definition puts himself on the other side of any barrier, fence or frontier we erect to safeguard what is our own or even what we think is his. [1]

The Wise Men represent then all humankind coming to worship the infant Jesus. In the twenty first century that means for me not aggressive evangelism but sharing the insights of Jesus – peace, justice, hope and love – with all people, and being prepared in turn to share the insights which their faith enshrines.

---

1 Colin Morris *Mankind my church* Hodder & Stoughton 1971 pp.73-74. I have placed in square brackets words I have changes in the interests of inclusive language.

The presentation of Christ in the temple

Luke 2.22-40, I Samuel 1.19-28, Romans 12.1–5

When does Christmas begin and end? One journalist wrote that for him it began when the mistletoe went up for the office party and ended when he returned at New Year after the Hogmanay hangover. For an American it began after Thanksgiving (the fourth Thursday in November) and ended on Super bowl Sunday in late January. A writer in *The Church Times* suggested that Christmas began with the first showing of *The Sound of Music* and ended with the last repeat of *The Vicar of Dibley*. No doubt we all have our own views.

But if the secular Christmas starts earlier and earlier then the church Christmas ends later and later. Our recently introduced Anglican calendar places greater emphasis on the season of Christmas, and it lasts until the 2nd February with the Presentation of Christ in the Temple, a celebration now promoted into the Premier League of Principal Feasts. It is that festival that we are celebrating today.

A threefold festival

It has three names and they are all drawn from the gospel we have just read.

The Purification of the Blessed Virgin Mary. In Jewish law set out in Leviticus 12, a poor woman should, 40 days after the birth of a male child, make an offering to the Lord of a pair of turtle doves and two young pigeons. And so Luke tells us that, 40 days after the birth of Jesus, Mary did just that.

The Presentation of Christ in the Temple. Again in accordance with Jewish practice described in Exodus 13, a first-born male child belonged to God and therefore needed to be redeemed. So the infant Jesus is brought to be presented to the Lord. Luke seems to have in mind the example of Hannah who brought the baby Samuel and presented him to the Lord as described in the Old Testament lesson from the first book of Samuel

Candlemas. Luke tells us how, following the presentation of Jesus, Mary and Joseph meet two old and devout people, one a man, Simeon and the other a woman, Anna, who recognise in the baby somebody special. (Luke has been described as the gospel of sexual equality: here he balances a man and a woman, Simeon and Anna.). Simeon describes Jesus as 'a light to lighten the Gentiles'. Candlemas didn't become a feast of the church until the fifth century. The practice grew up of celebrating Jesus as the light of the world by presenting worshippers with candles on this day. The candles were a visual aid to worship rather as we use ashes on Ash Wednesday and palm crosses on Palm Sunday. Candlemas was a name which disappeared at the Reformation because the reformers thought there were rather too many festivals associated with the Virgin Mary.

So today is the Purification of the Blessed Virgin Mary, the Presentation of Christ in the Temple and Candlemas. These are not among the popular and well known landmarks in the church calendar so what do they mean?

The nature of Jesus

The gospel passage we have just read is part of Luke's introduction where he highlights for us some of the themes which are to emerge as he goes on with the story of the life and death of Jesus. He tells us three things about Jesus.

Jesus was a good Jew. Luke has just told us that on the eighth day Jesus was circumcised. Now he tells us about the Purification of his mother and his presentation in the temple and he says three times in three verses 'all this was done according to the law of the Lord' – emphasising that Jesus had undergone all that Jewish faith required, an important message to Jews to whom the gospel was proclaimed. He says it again in verse 39; 'When they had finished everything required by the law of the Lord they returned to Galilee.' It was very important for the early Christians that Jesus should have been a faithful Jew: they valued the continuity of their faith from Judaism rather than seeing the two in opposition to each other. But it was also important that he was more than that.

Jesus was a universal saviour According to the aged Simeon this baby will be 'a light for revelation to the Gentiles' (Luke 2.32). At first sight this is very odd because Jesus ministry was directed chiefly to Jews. Only once did he heal a Gentile, the centurion's servant, described in Luke 7 (vv.2-10). Was Luke perhaps writing an introduction not just to his gospel but to his two-volume block-buster Luke-Acts? The first volume is about Jesus' ministry to Jews and it ends in Jerusalem, the Jewish city, with the death and Resurrection of Jesus. The second volume begins in Jerusalem, tells the story of the spread of a universal gospel and ends in Rome the capital of the known world.

Jesus would be a bringer of conflict It is not at all clear what Simeon's enigmatic words mean when he says 'This child is destined for the falling and rising of many in Israel ... a sword will pierce your own soul too' (2.34-35). Perhaps he means that many will reject the Messiah and that even Mary will experience the division which Jesus will cause. Luke recounts these words perhaps because they foreshadow one of the themes of his gospel – that of conflict. By the time he is writing, about 85AD, the Crucifixion lies in the past and conflicts in the early church are a reality.

So this story, told only by Luke, takes us back to the Old Testament, to Jewish law, to prophecy and forward to the future when Jesus will be both the glory of Israel and a light for revelation to the Gentiles, but will also bring division because some Jews will accept him as the Messiah while others will reject him.

'Present your bodies a living sacrifice'

But whenever we read the New Testament there is always another dimension. We ask first what did this passage mean to its first hearers? But we go on to ask what does it say to us reading it twenty centuries later and trying to live the Christian life? I want to suggest that for us the meaning of this passage is the call to present ourselves as an offering to God. In some sense all the participants in Luke's story were presenting themselves to God; not just the baby but his parents Mary and Joseph and the devout Simeon and Anna.

We read for our New Testament lesson the well-known words from Paul's letter to the Romans 'Present your bodies as a living sacrifice, holy and acceptable to God which is your spiritual worship'. And he goes on: 'Be not conformed to this world but be transformed by the renewing of your mind'. (Romans 12.1b & 2). Some of you will remember J.B.Phillips' translation of the New Testament letters called *Letters to Young Churches*. He has this translation of those words: 'Don't let the world squeeze you into its own mould, but let God remould you from within'. What then does presenting ourselves to God mean?

The Methodist Covenant service

On the first Sunday of each New Year Methodists join in the Covenant service. It is a service which has been adopted by other denominations and now often forms part of a New Year ecumenical service. It was introduced in 1755 by John Wesley as a service of rededication. Here are some words from it spoken by the congregation at the most solemn moment in the service:

> I am no longer my own but yours. Put me to what you will, rank me with whom you will; put me to doing, put me to suffering; let me be employed for you or laid aside for you, exalted for you or brought low for you; let me be full, let me be empty, let me have all things, let me have nothing; I freely and wholeheartedly yield all things to your pleasure and disposal. [1]

Searching and demanding words but perhaps catching a flavour of what it means to 'present our bodies a living sacrifice'.

- *Rank me with whom you will*: people of my own background, intelligence and interests, yes but also; people of different backgrounds, ethnic and social groups, contrary interests and points of view.
- *Put me to doing, put me to suffering*: let me be active, involved, busy; yes but also offered to you if I'm ill, incapacitated, handicapped or depressed.
- *Let me be employed for you or laid aside for you*: in an interesting and fulfilling job, yes of course but also compulsorily redundant, working unsocial hours, away from home and poorly paid.
- *Let me have all things, let me have nothing*: good salary, nice house, happy marriage, children I can be proud of – yes but also yours when I'm finding it hard to make ends meet, in poor health, separated or alone, children who are a constant anxiety.
- *I freely and wholeheartedly yield all things to your pleasure and disposal.*

'Don't let the world squeeze you into its own mould'. A mould, which recognises only success, health, happiness and finds it hard to cope with illness, death, failure, poverty, addiction and unhappiness. We are called to resist that mould and to live the Christian life in whatever conditions we find ourselves.

I recently watched a television programme about John Wells the well-known humorist. He was one of the funniest people of his generation, the person who invented Dear Bill in *Private Eye* for example. He died of a degenerative illness at the age of 62. He was a practising Christian. Moving tributes were paid to him by many people who said that visiting him during his last illness was an inspiration and a joy to the visitors. Never did he yield to self pity, he was never a sad or tragic figure but always amusing and good company. 'Let me be laid aside for you', says the Covenant Service.

Today then is the end of the Christmas season – the end of the time when we celebrate the coming of the Word made flesh. We finish this season with the presentation of a baby 40 days old in the Temple by his parents and 'we present our bodies'- our whole lives – 'a living sacrifice, holy, acceptable to God which is our spiritual worship'.

1. I have used the older version of the Covenant Service rather than the modern version. It can be found in *The Methodist Service Book 1975*

Evidence for the Resurrection

Blessed are those who have not seen and yet have come to believe
John 20. 29b

Easter has not been the same since the retirement of Dr David Jenkins, former Bishop of Durham in 1994. Each year while he was bishop, press, radio and television would gather round hoping that he would say something about the Resurrection of Jesus which was, in their view, incompatible with the status of a bishop and the faith of a Christian. He usually obliged. They would then demand his resignation, trial for heresy or burning at the stake. His offence was to ask the sort of question which any intelligent Christian, or indeed non-Christian, might ask about the raising of Jesus from the dead, an event which runs clean contrary to our experience of the physical world.

I want to discuss the evidence for the Resurrection and I do so in the light of the gospel we have just read, the account of Jesus' encounter after his Resurrection with Thomas, as it is described in John's gospel.

No account of the Resurrection only its consequences

Let me say first of all that the New Testament does not contain an account of the Resurrection. What is described is its outcome. No camera crew was there, no reporter claimed to have been an eyewitness. Jesus's followers met him in various places on Easter day and in the weeks following his death; they believed the tomb was empty and their subsequent lives were transformed. But all these things were consequences of an event which none of them observed.

Let me speak briefly about each of the three strands of evidence.

The Resurrection appearances

Each of the four gospels contains accounts of appearances of Jesus to his followers. They cannot, incidentally, be harmonised with each other so that there are no discrepancies, despite the well-known attempt to do so in Frank Morison's book *Who moved the stone?* first published in 1930. There are for example significant differences between the accounts of the first Easter morning in each of the four gospels.

Jesus appears to a variety of people – to Mary of Magdala, Mary the mother of James, to Salome, Peter and John, to Thomas and Nathanael, to Cleopas and his companion on the road to Emmaus, and, according to St

Paul, to about 500 people together, most of whom, he tells us, were still alive when he was writing over 20 years later. Jesus appears at different times of the day – while it was still dark, at daybreak, in the evening – and in different places – at the tomb, by the Sea of Galilee, in an upper room in Jerusalem and on the road to Emmaus.

But there is mystery about the appearances. What sort of appearances were they and what was the body of the Risen Lord like? Luke says he ate a piece of broiled fish (24.42), John says he appeared when all the doors were locked (20.19). 'Touch me and see' he said to his disciples Luke 24.39). 'Place your hands in the print of the nails' he said to Thomas (John 20.27). So his risen body had both human and supernatural characteristics. There is however reticence about his appearances: they are not such as to overwhelm or coerce. He was not at once recognised. In Mark's account it is a young man in a white robe who tells the women that Jesus has risen (16.5). According to Luke Cleopas and his friend walk for miles with him before recognising that the stranger is Jesus (24.16, 31). In John's account Mary mistakes him for the gardener (20.15). The fact that he is risen must it appears be absorbed and accepted by each, gently and gradually.

Nor were the appearances such as to convince opponents. Jesus appeared to those who were already his followers; there is no appearance to convince Pilate or persuade the Chief Priests.

The empty tomb

The second strand of evidence is the empty tomb. Each of the gospels tells us that the tomb was empty, though the earliest account, that of Paul in the First Letter to the Corinthians does not mention it. There is evidence too in the gospels that other explanations of the empty tomb were circulating. Matthew tells how the guards were paid to spread the story that the disciples had stolen the body, and he adds, the Jews tell this story 'to this day', which must have been over 50 years after the Resurrection. According to John's account, Mary thought the authorities might have moved the body: 'They have taken my lord out of the tomb and we do not know where they have laid him' (20.2). And yet neither Jews nor Romans produced the body even though this would have been the conclusive way of scotching the rumour that he had risen.

But of course for us in the twentieth century there is a deeper problem. 'What happened to the body', we inevitably ask. Once blood has ceased to circulate, tissue degenerates at once and there is irreversible brain damage. So resurrection or resuscitation of a corpse presents difficulties. It is the problem to which Bishop Jenkins drew attention arguing that for him the truth of the Resurrection did not depend on an empty tomb. For some of us there is no problem; the Resurrection of Jesus is a miracle. Of course it breaches the natural order, that is the nature of miracle, even if we do not know how it was accomplished. For others, the more sceptical among us, David Jenkins' questions remain. The truth is that we shall never know exactly what happened. For some faith and the evidence of the gospels tells them the tomb was empty and that his body was raised, others can only maintain a reverent agnosticism at this point. But in either case the truth of the Resurrection does not depend on the empty tomb.

The life of the church

There is a third strand of evidence to set alongside the Resurrection appearances and the empty tomb – the transformation of the disciples. The gospels describe how the arrest, trial and crucifixion of Jesus left his followers in dismay and disarray. Peter denies that he knew him and the others run away leaving a stranger, Joseph of Arimathea to bury Jesus. When Jesus appears they are to be found skulking behind locked doors and some have returned to their old job as fishermen.

Yet within a matter of weeks they are changed people. They meet, no longer as Jews did on the Sabbath day, but on the first day of the week, which they now call the Lord's Day. They hold a meal together to remember him, but not a solemn requiem on Thursday to recall the final meal with him, nor on Friday to commemorate his death but a meal of thanksgiving and rejoicing, a Eucharist, on the Lord's Day to celebrate his Resurrection, before they go off to work or when they return in the evening. The people, the meal, the day are all evidence for the Resurrection. But so is their life, both separately and together. Within weeks of the Resurrection they are prepared to endure persecution and even suffer martyrdom and their common life exhibits the supernatural love of which Paul speaks so eloquently in the first letter to the Corinthians chapter 13.

But the evidence didn't end with those first followers. Christians and the life of the church ever since bear witness to the Resurrection. And so of course we are part of the evidence. For about two thirds of the whole existence of the church there has been worship here in Bishop's Waltham. That we are here on the Lord's Day, sharing this same meal, and the supernatural life of the church is the result of what happened on that first Easter Day.

'Jesus Christ raised from the dead – fact of history', said the Wayside Pulpit. Wrong. Jesus raised from the dead is not a fact of history, not something which can be verified by the ordinary rules of historical evidence. Jesus Christ crucified is a fact of history, something which could be observed by anybody who happened to be in Jerusalem on Good Friday. But the Resurrection was and is known by faith not by unaided reason.

Let me conclude with a quotation from Alan Richardson, sometime Professor of Christian Theology at the University of Nottingham and later Dean of York.

'The principal argument for the truth of Christ's Resurrection does not consist of a skilful piecing together of the documentary evidence of the Gospels, or even of the New Testament as a whole, but in what the church does every Sunday and in the quality of her life on every day of the week.[1]

Evidence for the Resurrection is provided by the appearances to his followers and by the empty tomb but the proof of the Resurrection is simply us and the worldwide church of which we are part – our worship and our life together in the Body of Christ. *Blessed are those who have not seen and yet have come to believe.*

So we respond to the Easter greeting 'Christ is Risen, Alleluia!' with our own 'He is risen indeed. Alleluia'.

1. Alan Richardson *An introduction to the theology of the New Testament* SCM 1958 p.190

The journey to Emmaus

Luke 24.13-35

I went recently to an exhibition at the National Gallery. It was entitled *Caravaggio, the final years.* Caravaggio was an Italian painter who lived a stormy life and died at the age of 38 in 1610. The exhibition consisted of 16 remarkable paintings most of them of well known Biblical scenes. It started with two arresting pictures of *The Supper at Emmaus,* one painted in 1601 and the other in 1606. In the first Jesus was shown at the supper table with hands uplifted blessing the food – bread, wine, a basket of fruit and a plate of cold chicken. The travellers were two middle aged men, with abundant dark hair and beards, each showing by body language and gesture their amazement and excitement at the event which they are witnessing. One had his arms outstretched, the other, his back to us, was straining forward in his chair.

The story of the journey to Emmaus told only by Luke is perhaps the best known and most loved of all the Resurrection stories in the gospels. It may have been based on a true incident – though nobody has identified the village of Emmaus – but Luke has made it more than that. He wrote for people who were living the Christian life, perhaps in conditions of difficulty, even persecution. The Emmaus story is a parable of how the risen lord was encountered by people living many years later. It served the purpose not of history but of celebration, not of memorial but of living.

Let me draw your attention to four stages of the journey.

The journey begins in perplexity

Cleopas and his unnamed companion, perhaps his wife, though according to Caravaggio, the companions were men, ordinary village craftsmen, are travelling home from Jerusalem to a village called Emmaus. They are sad and disillusioned. They have met Jesus, perhaps heard him teach and seen him heal; they may have been in the crowd round the cross. They had great expectations of him: 'We had been hoping that he was the man to liberate Israel'. He was the key to their need for meaning in life. But their hopes have been dashed and they are sad. They had heard rumours of the Resurrection but they could simply not get their minds round such a strange reversal. Only two days ago they had seen him die and death is final.

The accepted interpretation is that anybody who doubts the Resurrection is a Doubting Thomas or perhaps a Doubting Cleopas. Yet the dominant note of the gospel accounts is of disbelief and astonishment. And that should not surprise us. The Resurrection is not easy to believe. If it is not a problem to us at least some of the time we have perhaps lost sight of what a unique and awe-inspiring event it is.

It never seems to have occurred to the Emmaus travellers that their companion was other than a man of flesh and blood, a visitor to Jerusalem. When later they discover who he is they conclude that some mysterious restraint had prevented them recognising him. Does Jesus I wonder encounter us in people of flesh and blood in whom we fail to recognise the divine spark?

Let's return to the state of mind of the travellers. Their disillusionment resonates with us. This is where the journey begins. The journey to faith or in faith often includes hopes which do not materialise, expectations which are not realised. Most people's journey includes relationships which don't work out, career plans which are disappointed, suffering which seems pointless, expectations which are not fulfilled and even God who appears to let us down. Many people will tell you that their Christian faith began with just such perplexity, that it grew from a sense of emptiness. Christians will sometimes confess that their journey is still frequently marked by perplexity, not just at its beginning but on the way. We perhaps need to recognise this stage in the journey in our own experience and that of those whom we hope might join us in the journey of faith.

The journey continues in dialogue

The heart of the Emmaus story is a dialogue between Cleopas and his companion and the unrecognised stranger. Events which to them are so vivid are to him apparently unknown, yet he seems capable of drawing from them the matters which preoccupy them.

'What are you discussing with each other while you walk along?' says the stranger
'Are you the only person who doesn't know the things that have happened?' they reply.
'What things?' he says.
'The things about Jesus of Nazareth' they respond.

Recognising the Risen Lord involves a process of dialogue. God invites us to take our questions to him. He shows a sympathy and awareness of our predicament even when we find it hard to express. He does not provide ready-made answers but invites us to ask further questions and to listen. Coming to faith begins with the awareness that we are listened to, that our questions are not naive, unreasonable or impertinent. And the questions do not cease when we come to faith: the dialogue with the Lord is part of the journey. We often pose questions to each other in fellowship and find answers which seem to come not just from each other but from God.

The journey leads to recognition

Recognition in the story takes two forms. First, Jesus interprets the Old Testament scriptures. 'Beginning with Moses and all the prophets he interpreted to them the things about himself in all the scriptures'. Not a handful of proof texts strung together without pattern or purpose, something of which we are sometimes guilty. He shows them that what has just happened in Jerusalem is not a failure, not an inexplicable disaster but part of the pattern of God's plan for his people. The mystery of suffering, failure, and frustration are to us often impediments to faith. Recognition is that even suffering can make sense, that life has an overall pattern and purpose. Notice too that what Jesus reveals is a Biblical pattern of redemptive suffering, an overall picture of what the story of the Jews in the Old Testament is all about.

But the second recognition is far more profound; it is recognition not simply of pattern and purpose but of a person. The two travellers reach Emmaus; their still unknown companion seems to be going further; they urge him to stay; they prepare a meal; he sits down to eat with them but he becomes the host; he takes the bread, gives thanks, breaks it and gives it to them. They suddenly recognise him. The Caravaggio picture makes Jesus the dominant figure at the meal, the host not the guest. Almost at once he vanishes.

There is enough in those few sentences for a lifetime of meditation.

- He always seems to be going ahead of us; to be with us yet beyond us.
- We urge him to stay – he only stays at our invitation. We want to possess him, to reduce him to our dimensions. We try to imprison him in a building, in our liturgy, in our church life, in our understanding of what it is to be a Christian, in our good works even.
- He is recognised in an ordinary meal, in the events of daily life.
- It is an experience which is too intense and he vanishes. The essence of the Christian way is to know him by faith not by sight.
- Is the meal also a Eucharist? It has obvious eucharistic overtones – the fourfold action of taking, giving thanks, breaking and distributing is what we do in each Eucharist. It is one of the things which leads me to say that the story is a parable – it presupposes the experience of the Eucharist in the lives of believers which would not have happened a mere three days after the Last Supper.
- And what is the relation between recognition of Jesus in ordinary life and in weekly worship?

The journey ends in response

He vanishes. What do Cleopas and his companion – man or woman – do now – wash up, lay the breakfast, go to bed? Surely not. They are tired, it is late, Jerusalem is seven miles away but there is no alternative- they have to tell somebody. So back they go. I wonder what they talked about on the return journey or were they silent, wrapped in amazement at what had happened? They find the eleven and their companions gathered together.

They too had met the Lord. They recounted their experience and how he had been made known to them in the breaking of the bread. Emmaus is a country retreat; Jerusalem is where the action is.

The experience of recognising the Risen Lord is not a piece of abstract information to be kept to ourselves. It is to be shared. But that may mean a variety of things. It includes the whole of Christian living. It was at Jerusalem and because of the Risen Lord that the church began. It was here that 2000 years of life and witness started.

The journey to Emmaus is then one for all of us – enquirer, fringe member, and committed believer alike. But the stages of the journey – perplexity, dialogue, recognition and response – are not an orderly progression, not a once for all, but repeated throughout life. We are always on a journey perhaps simultaneously on each part of it. Our Christian lives are at the same time characterised by perplexity, dialogue, recognition and response, indeed we should not be surprised if sometimes they seem to get stuck at perplexity and scarcely reach response.

Ascension

They went back to Jerusalem full of joy. Luke 24.52
Jesus Christ is the same yesterday, today and forever. Hebrews 13.8

The city of York where I worked for three years in the early 1990s is full of tourists all the year round. Many of them are Americans whose voices are rarely muted and whose appreciation of what they are seeing is trumpeted for all to hear. One afternoon I followed a group of Americans round Fairfax House, a superb seventeenth century building in the centre of the city which had recently been restored. One lady summed up her feelings at the end. 'Very nice' she said ' but very old'. Now that is just what many people would say about Jesus. 'A very good man but very old'. Or to put it another way, a good man trapped in the first century AD and therefore with not much to say to the twenty first century. Now Christians acknowledge that Jesus was a first century man but we also believe that he transcends time and place. The Ascension which we celebrate today is the hinge which holds these two together.

There are two problems which confront any modern person considering the Ascension.

A three-storey universe

The imagery of the Ascension assumes a three-storey universe. It was easy for a first century person who believed the earth was flat to think of Jesus making a journey from earth up to a localised heaven 'beyond the bright blue sky'. But for us it is impossible. We know why the sky is blue, that the earth is not flat and that if you go up 30,000 feet you do not come to a sort of celestial attic because we have been there courtesy of British Airways. So the vision of Jesus floating upwards is frankly embarrassing and indeed incredible.

The Ascension only described in Acts

But second it is only Luke who puts the departure of Jesus in this way and only in Acts that he describes the Ascension: 'As they were watching, he was lifted up and a cloud took him out of their sight' (1.9). In the other gospels there is no moment of parting. In his gospel Luke puts the departure of Jesus on Easter Day and describes it like this: 'Then he led them out as far as Bethany, and, lifting up his hands, he blessed them. While he was blessing them, he withdrew from them and was carried up into heaven'. (24.50–51) (These last words 'and was carried up to heaven', are not included in many manuscripts.)[1]

But the idea of Jesus' post-Resurrection appearances ceasing is common to all the gospels and to the New Testament letters. The writers used a variety of words and phrases to describe this climax of gospel history. The New Testament is full of references to Jesus 'being exalted', and 'sitting down at the right hand of God'. But we have no idea how he got there. 'What actually happened', says John Habgood, former Archbishop of York, 'was not a question which the evangelists had any interest in answering'.

The Ascension stands then for the truth that the earthly life of Jesus was over and that he would in future be experienced by his followers in an entirely new way. It marks the transition from the outward companionship which his followers had experienced while he was with them to the inward communion with him which we share. There are two phrases which express this new way and which I want to explore: from sight to faith and from yesterday to today.

From sight to faith

Have you noticed how each of the gospel accounts of the Resurrection has a similar ending? There is no prolonged encounter with any of those who met Jesus after the Resurrection. Each meeting is brief. Mary already in tears recognises that the person whom she has met is Jesus only when he says her name. Her instinctive desire is to embrace him. And Jesus says at once 'Do not hold on to me.' (John 20.17). Thomas demands to see the print of the nails but the point of the encounter is made by Jesus, 'Blessed are those who have not seen and yet have come to believe'. (John 20.29) The travellers to Emmaus recognise him as he breaks bread – and at once he vanishes. (Luke 24.31)

Mary must meet the ascended Lord not cling to the man who is speaking to her. Thomas is pointed to a faith independent of physical evidence. The travellers to Emmaus must learn that he is always there when the scriptures are opened and the bread broken.

The Ascension is the culminating lesson. In some way the disciples realise that they will never see Jesus again. Luke describes their response in what is to me one of the most astonishing verses in the whole Bible: ' They returned to Jerusalem full of joy'. (Luke 24.52) It is as though we were to describe a funeral as a joyful occasion. They will never see him again but they rejoice at this final departure – only because it is not an end but a beginning.

From sight to faith and second – from yesterday to today.

From yesterday to today

When he was on earth Jesus was known to few people in one small country in a corner of the world. His teaching was heard by few, the impact of his personality was restricted to those who met him. I wonder how many people could claim to have met and talked to Jesus – a few hundred or perhaps a thousand even but no more. But the ascended Christ is quite different. His influence on world history is incalculable. It has been felt by more people than any other person in the whole of recorded history.

The book of Hebrews contains one of the best-known verses in the Bible ' Jesus Christ, the same yesterday, today and forever' (13.8). It is something which cannot be said about any other person. Plato, Socrates, Julius Caesar, St Francis of Assisi, Nelson, Gandhi, Winston Churchill have all influenced human history but all of them are restricted by the era in which they lived. They are tied to a given century and to a small part of the world. Jesus has been portrayed as white, black and yellow, in the clothes of the ancient world, and the medieval world and as our contemporary. He has spoken equally to St Paul, St Augustine, Luther, Mother Theresa, and Desmond Tutu and to you and me. He inspired those who spent their last days hiding in the catacombs, those who faced almost certain death taking the gospel to Africa, the slave trader John Newton and the Tory philanthropist Lord Shaftsbury.

But we must be clear what it means to speak of Jesus the same, yesterday, today and forever. It means that he is our contemporary, speaking in our language to our culture. He is a figure of the present not of the past. Let me illustrate.

Castle Drogo, often described as the last castle erected in England, was built in the early years of the twentieth century. The architect was Edwin Lutyens and it is situated on a superb site on the edge of Dartmoor. It is now owned by the National Trust. As you go round the castle you will see a bedroom which belonged to the eldest son of the man who commissioned the castle, Adrian Drewe, a young man who was killed at Ypres in 1916. His school photographs are on the wall, his Oxford BA gown hangs on the door, his diaries and sepia tinted photos of family and friends are scattered around. The room has been left exactly as he last lived in it before he went off to the trenches in France. It is almost unbearably evocative of the golden years before 1914 and the tragedy of the First World War.

But this is exactly what our memory of Jesus must not be. He lives not by being insulated from time and change but by participating in them. His story is renewed in each generation by a deep understanding of him and of what he is as our contemporary. Any institution which fails to change whether it is the monarchy, parliament or the church slowly dies. The Ascension is the sign that Jesus lives and changes in order to speak to each generation and in each part of the world.

On 17th July 1966 a great congregation assembled in St Peter's Cathedral in Geneva. Members of the congregation were Christian leaders from all over the world attending a World Council of Churches conference on Church and Society. The most striking feature of the service was that during the sermon the pulpit was empty. The preacher was heard in hushed silence even though he was not visible. His name was Martin Luther King. He had felt obliged to cancel his visit to Geneva to be in Chicago to mediate in the race riots then at their height. But even more powerful than his sermon was the symbol of his absence living the gospel he was preaching

That image conveys to me something of the mystery and power of the Ascension, the Jesus who is present equally in first century Palestine and in our twenty first century world, the Jesus who is present in church as we worship but equally at work in the world where we spend most of our lives.

1. See the note appended to this verse in NRSV.

Pentecost – the birthday of the church

Genesis 11.1–9, Acts 2.1–21.

Preachers are advised to gain the attention of their congregation at the beginning of the sermon. I recall the – no doubt apocryphal – story of the young lady Methodist local preacher who was taking morning and evening services at the village chapel. In the morning she preached to a sparse congregation sitting on the side of the pulpit with her legs dangling over the side. News spread round the village and in the evening the chapel was packed with people hoping to see the preacher's shapely legs. She preached a powerful, evangelical sermon but to the chagrin of her congregation with her legs securely hidden behind the oak pulpit.

The birthday of the church

This morning I recall the story of the young curate who mounted the pulpit steps on Pentecost Sunday, raised his arms above his head, shouted *Many happy returns,* to his astonished congregation and led them in a rousing chorus of *Happy Birthday to You.* Not only did the young curate gain the attention of his congregation but he was right. Pentecost is not as we often think the story of the first coming of the Holy Spirit – that is recorded in the second verse of the first chapter of Genesis. Pentecost is Luke's account of the coming of the Holy Spirit to the followers of Jesus after the Resurrection: the birthday of the church.

Acts chapter 2 contains Luke's account of events which changed a scattered, demoralised and bewildered collection of the followers of Jesus into a community of faith which has lasted almost 2000 years and is to be found in every country on earth. It is the presence and power of the Holy Spirit which converted this group of very ordinary people into the church. Luke tells us the story of Pentecost at the beginning of his second volume because he is going to recount some of the things which the Spirit enabled the church to do in the first few years of its existence.

Three images of the Spirit

Acts chapter 2 is an extraordinarily rich chapter with a whole lot of hints about the nature and life of the infant church. The experience of those early

Christians at Pentecost was so powerful that it cannot be captured in words. Not even the most skilful use of language will do justice to the experiences of that day. And so Luke uses symbols to convey his meaning.

- The disciples hear a sound like wind, he says, – not a gentle breeze or an ordinary wind but a sound which he describes as 'like the rush of a violent wind' – a gale in fact (v.2).
- They see something they can only describe as 'divided tongues as of fire' (v.3) with a tongue resting on each of them – not real flames but a sight which can best be captured in the dramatic image of fire.
- They begin to speak strangely so that according to Luke 'each one heard them speaking the native language of each'(v. 6) another unprecedented phenomenon.

The Spirit of power

This chapter is so familiar to us that we may well have missed just how powerful are the images it uses – a gale force wind, tongues of fire and unfamiliar languages. But there is a more serious problem. As a result of not taking these New Testament images seriously we have tamed the Spirit. We think of the Holy Spirit as the Comforter – indeed the collect this morning prays that *We may rejoice in his holy comfort*. In the well-known Pentecost hymn we sing *And his that gentle voice we hear, soft as the breath of even*. Now I'm sure we all know that comfort comes from two Latin words *con fortis* meaning 'with strength'. But I suspect that we still think of comfort as the dictionary defines it as 'a state of ease and well being'. The Spirit is surely not sent to enable the church to experience a state of ease and well being. It is precisely because the Spirit comes so powerfully, as a gale, as fire and as strange speech that the church has survived persecution and produced martyrs from the first century to the twentieth. It has witnessed in Nero's Rome, in Hitler's Germany and in Idi Amin's Uganda.

That is the first thing I want to say this morning. The Spirit of Pentecost is a Spirit of power.

The Spirit of unity and reconciliation

Second I want to explore further one, and perhaps the strangest, of Luke's three signs of the Spirit's presence, speech in languages strange to both speakers and hearers. On the day of Pentecost, we are told, those who listened to the disciples each heard them speaking in their own language – Parthians, Medes, Elamites, people who lived in Mesopotamia, Egypt,

Libya, Rome and Crete, – people from all round the Mediterranean and beyond – all heard the wonderful works of God in their own language (Acts 2. 8-11).

What I wonder do you make of that? What on earth was going on? Did they really speak all those languages? Even the Holy Spirit could scarcely teach them the grammar, syntax and vocabulary of one unfamiliar language, let alone several, in an instant. So I'm sceptical about the literal truth of what Luke has to say.

It seems more likely that Pentecost was an example of speaking in tongues or *glossolalia*, to which there are references later in Acts and in the first letter to the Corinthians. It takes place when an intense religious experience leads people to utter worship and praise to God in words and sounds which are beyond ordinary human speech. Words don't matter; sense is conveyed through a shared experience which carries people beyond the limitations of their own language into a universal language of worship and praise. It still happens in some Christian communions today. You may have experienced speaking in tongues or know people who have done. For some people it is an authentic way of experiencing the power of the Spirit. Paul recognises its existence but has some reservations.

Let me however suggest an explanation which brings Pentecost nearer the experience of all of us. We can all think of occasions when words are wholly inadequate to express what we feel. When we want to convey how much we love somebody, when we need to express profound joy or deep sorrow, when we want to sympathise with somebody in bereavement, words can be pitifully inadequate. They seem superfluous, trivial, and intrusive or even a barrier to communication. A sympathetic eye, a warm cuddle are often so much better. If you have tried to write a letter of sympathy, or read somebody else's love letters with embarrassment, you will know what I mean. So perhaps the disciples of Jesus on the day of Pentecost had such a profound sense of joy and peace and power that they conveyed the message without needing ordinary words and the writer expresses that by saying that they all heard in their own language. And that is supported by the observation that some people thought they were drunk – they were beside themselves with joy.

That experience of unity, joy and mutual sharing in the gospel, which is the gift of the Spirit, is available to us at a level deeper than human language. The party which went from this deanery to the diocese of Calabar in eastern Nigeria, of which I was a member, often could not understand fully what was said to us but we were in no doubt of our unity in the gospel. We experienced a sort of Pentecost. We differed in so many ways – black and white, rich and poor, the first world, the two thirds world, clothes, customs, culture, history, experience – couldn't have been more different. But there was a supernatural unity created by the Spirit. We heard the same gospel each in our own language. But you don't need to go to Nigeria to experience the Spirit in that way. In some sense we experience the gift of the Spirit, the gift of unity and joy and love every time we come to worship.

Pentecost reverses Babel

But the commentators have another suggestion to make about the meaning of the Pentecost story. The Old Testament lesson for Pentecost is from Genesis chapter 11, the strange story of the Tower of Babel. It is a myth of human arrogance. The families of Noah build a city with a tower which reaches to heaven. And God says, 'I will cut you down to size. Because of your arrogance, you will no longer speak a single language. You are united in your self-sufficiency; in future you will be scattered and unable to communicate with each other. You will be at war with one another.'(based on vv.6-9)

Babel stands for human kind – its disobedience, its over weaning pride, its divisions. And if you want evidence of the profound truth of the Babel myth look around – Ireland, Israel, the Balkans, Kashmir, or the appalling history of the twentieth century. We seem incapable of communicating with each other in the language of a common humanity. We do not have a language either spoken or unspoken in which we can resolve our differences and live together in harmony. Every civilisation is in the eyes of God a tower of Babel. As human beings we refuse to curb our ambitions and accept our place in nature: through our over-weaning pride we desecrate the world God has given us.

But, say the commentators, the significance of Pentecost is that it reverses Babel. God's gift is unity, a common language, not a religious Esperanto, but unity in obedience, unity in service, unity in worship. The Spirit can recreate humanity as one great family. It is for this reason that the disunity of the church is such a scandal – because it is contrary to the gift God gives at Pentecost, the gift of unity, of speaking in a single language.

Let me draw the threads together. Pentecost is the birthday of the church: the church was constituted and lives by the Spirit.

- The Spirit is a spirit of power – like a gale force wind.
- The Spirit, to quote the words of the Preface for Pentecost in the Eucharistic prayer, 'unites peoples of many tongues in one faith'. He is the Spirit of unity between Christians.

- The Spirit reverses Babel and is the means of reconciliation between peoples.

I finish with a quotation from one of the great devotional masterpieces of the twentieth century sadly neglected these days – William Temple's *Readings in St John's Gospel* [1]

> When we pray 'Come Holy Ghost, our souls inspire', we had better know what we are about. He will not carry us to easy triumphs and gratifying successes; more probably he will set us some task for God in the full intention that we shall fail, so that others, learning wisdom by our failure, may carry the good cause forward.... If we invoke him we must be ready for the glorious pain of being caught by his power out of our petty orbit into the eternal purposes of the Almighty. ...

And he concludes: 'Come then Great Spirit, come. Convict the world; and convict my timid soul.'

1 William Temple *Readings in St John's gospel* Macmillan Complete edition 945 p.288

Trinity

Through Christ we have access to the Father by the one Spirit.
Ephesians 2.18

A defence of theology

Harold Wilson, who was Prime Minister in the 1960s and 70s, often used the word theology though he applied it not to religion but to politics. He was dismissive of theology. He meant by it theory divorced from practice, nit picking abstractions as opposed to the stuff of everyday life. There are plenty of people in the church who have a similar view of theology in its religious sense. (There is of course theology studied in universities which need be no more relevant to daily life than academic economics is to the average person shopping in a supermarket.) But there is a theology which is a description of the Christian life and serves to deepen faith and understanding and that is something which we ought to take seriously. Theology in this sense ought not to be the preserve of clergy and the more erudite laity but should be accessible to all of us.

Today is Trinity Sunday when we turn to the central mystery of the Christian faith, the belief that God is best described as a Trinity, three persons and yet one God. Now there are few doctrines which are apparently more complex, abstruse and theoretical. And yet it is central to Christian belief. In recent years the Trinity has made something of a comeback in our liturgy. After 20 years in which we spoke of 'Sundays after Pentecost', *Common Worship* has reverted to 'Sundays after Trinity'. We are bidden too to introduce the intercessions at the Eucharist with the sentence 'In the power of the Spirit and in union with Christ, let us pray to the Father'. The collects are now offered 'through Jesus Christ our Lord, who is alive and reigns with you in the unity of the Holy Spirit, one God now and for ever', a bit of a mouthful though no doubt theologically impeccable.

A doctrine not found in the New Testament

But the doctrine of the Trinity remains difficult for many of us. The first problem is that there is no doctrine of the Trinity in the Bible. We have just read two short passages from the New Testament which appear to speak of the Trinity. The first is at the end of Matthew's gospel where Jesus commands the disciples to baptise in the name of the Father and of the Son and of the Holy Spirit. (28.19). The second is at the end of Paul's second letter to the Corinthians where he signs off with the words familiar to us as the Grace: 'The grace of our Lord Jesus Christ, the love of God and the communion of the Holy Spirit be with all of you'(13.14). But these may not be part of the original New Testament and in any case contain no doctrine of the Trinity – no exposition or explanation of it. There are passages where the doctrine of the Trinity is implicit but nowhere where it is explicit. It was not until the fourth century that the doctrine was fully developed and not until the tenth century that Trinity Sunday was first celebrated. In England it was popularised by Thomas a Becket who you recall was murdered in Canterbury Cathedral in 1170.

All of which leads me to conclude that any preacher on Trinity Sunday has a tough assignment. I want this morning to try and answer two questions – how did the church arrive at the Trinity and how do we experience God as the Trinity today?

How did the early church arrive at the Trinity?

The doctrine of the Trinity was formulated in the fourth century at a time when controversy about Christian teaching was as fierce and as much debated as the merits of rival football teams or pop groups are today. The thought world of the fourth century was radically different from that of the twenty first century. For example when we talk about God as three persons we think of three separate entities or separate bodies. In the fourth century person was much closer to 'modes of being'. So you might say that you and I are three persons because we have memory, understanding and will. That doesn't mean that we are three people but only that we need these three attributes in order to be complete persons: we are all of us one in three and three in one. We are dealing with a different use of words to describe a common experience.

Let me go back to the experience of the early church as they tried to understand and describe their Christian lives and in particular how their experience of Christ fitted into their knowledge of God. Many of them were Jews. Their God was the God of the Old Testament. He was the creator and upholder of the universe, the God of Abraham, Isaac and Jacob. He had brought them out of bondage in Egypt and delivered them from captivity in Babylon. Over against the shrines, cults and holy places of their neighbours he was one. Through the synagogue on the Sabbath rang the words known to the Jews as the Schema: ' Hear O Israel the Lord our God, the Lord is one'(Deuteronomy 6. 4).

It was into this Jewish world that Jesus came. To his followers he was more than an ordinary human being. He had spoken with unique authority. They believed a new age had dawned with his coming. Above all he had been raised from the dead and they experienced his life inspiring them. They could neither believe in two Gods nor could they deny their experience of Jesus so they enlarged their description of God. He was 'the God and Father of our Lord Jesus Christ'.

The Holy Spirit was to them not an impersonal force. He was the person through whom Jesus was alive and present, the person through whom God guided them, in whose strength they lived, witnessed and died. The Spirit enabled them to show qualities unattainable in any other way. The Holy Spirit they concluded was one of God's permanent ways of being God. It was natural that they should baptise their converts in the name of the Father and the Son and the Holy Spirit. The Christian life was finding and doing the Father's will expressed in the person of Jesus Christ through the guidance and strength of the Holy Spirit.

To summarise: the early Christians could not separate their experience of Father, Son and Holy Spirit, all three were ways in which they knew God. They could not subordinate one to the others nor deny that God was one. It was Ian Ramsey, bishop of Durham and before that a noted philosopher of religion, until his sadly early death, who said ' Christians could not get along with the single word God. Their richer and fuller experience demanded a more complex symbol for its expression. Their Trinity was not an abstruse doctrine but a description of the God they worshipped and served.'

How do we experience the Trinity?

We are often told that 70% of people in England believe in God. There are two questions which follow – What do they mean by God? What difference does it make? A Yorkshire man once expressed his belief in God like this –'There's a sort of summat somewhere'. Would it I wonder have made much difference if he had said – 'There's 'nowt nowhere'? When we say we believe in God we mean that we believe in the God whom we see at work in Jesus Christ and experience in our lives through the Holy Spirit. In other words our God is God the Holy Trinity.

In 1985 there was a very serious fire at York Minster shortly after the consecration of David Jenkins as bishop of Durham. He had achieved notoriety shortly beforehand by expressing doubts about the Virgin Birth and the bodily Resurrection of Jesus. Some people said that God had set the Minster on fire to indicate his displeasure at the consecration of David Jenkins. I know that is not the case because a God liable to lose his temper and demonstrate his displeasure by setting fire to a Gothic masterpiece would not be the God and Father of our Lord Jesus Christ.

More recently it has been suggested that the AIDS epidemic was a sign of God's anger about homosexuals or drug abusers or both. I know otherwise because a God who could inflict misery on women and children as well as gay people would not be the God and Father of our Lord Jesus Christ. The God of earthquake and famine, the God who slew the priests of Baal is not the God whom we know through Jesus Christ.

Some pretty odd things have been claimed in the name of the Holy Spirit too. There was for example the man who threw himself off the tower of Notre Dame cathedral in Paris because the Spirit told him to. People will sometimes claim to be guided by the Spirit to do things which are irrational, idiosyncratic or just plain stupid. How then do we recognise what the Spirit is saying to us and ensure that it is not just a projection of what we wanted to do all along? Because the Spirit speaks what is in conformity with what we know already of God the Father through Jesus Christ.

Let me summarise what I have tried to say this morning. First, the Trinity is the only idea of God which did justice to the experience of the early church. Second, it is the only idea of God which makes sense of his dealings with us. The doctrine of the Trinity came about to describe, define and safeguard the Christian experience of God.

But the Trinity is still a mystery but that surely is what you would expect of the nature of God. I finish with the last verse of Isaac Watts' great hymn on the Trinity and particularly the last two lines.

> Almighty God to Thee
> Be endless honours done,
> The undivided Three,
> And the mysterious One.
> *Where reason fails with all her powers,*
> *There faith prevails and love adores.*[1]

1. *Common Praise* Canterbury press 2000 Number 206

All Saints and All Souls

Paul a servant of Jesus Christ …to all God's people in Rome,
who are called to be saints. Romans 1.1&7

I was brought up proud to be a Protestant. It is not I'm afraid a word you often hear in the Church of England today. The word Protestant was first used in 1529 but it soon became the general term for the followers of the reformers of whom the most prominent were Martin Luther and John Calvin. They rejected the corruption of the late medieval church and wanted to return to a simpler and more biblical faith. I was brought up a Protestant so you will not be surprised that I have reservations about both the festivals which our calendar bids us celebrate this weekend. Yesterday 1st November was All Saints' day and today 2nd November is All Souls' day. Why first are there two very similar festivals and on consecutive days?

Two festivals

Early in the history of the church local churches remembered those who had died for their faith on the anniversary of their death. The first we know of is Polycarp bishop of Smyrna who died in 155 AD. By the fourth century the qualification for sainthood was reduced from martyrdom to sanctity. You no longer had to die for your faith. Those who had lived particularly good lives could also qualify as saints. But there were some whose date of death was not known so All Saints' day was introduced to cover them. Since about the year 730 All Saints' day has been celebrated on 1st November. Perhaps I should add that it was not until the twelfth century that the pope got his hands on the canonisation procedure. Pope John Paul II canonised more saints during his twenty-four year pontificate than all his predecessors combined since the current procedure was adopted in 1588.

All Souls' day originated in Spain in the seventh century but was not fixed at 2nd November until 998, by the great monastery of Cluny in Burgundy. It was a day on which to remember all those who had died in the faith, whether their lives were particularly virtuous or not. All Saints' day was for the great and the good, All Souls' day for the ordinary and the obscure. The idea behind All Souls' was that the prayers of the saints in paradise could help to secure remission of days, weeks or years in purgatory for the faithful. It was naturally enough dropped from the calendar of the Church of England at the Reformation when belief in purgatory was abandoned as un-Biblical. It returned in the *Alternative Service Book* in 1980. The Thirty Nine Articles had no doubt that the Bible knew nothing of purgatory. This is what it had to say about it in Article 22. 'The Romish doctrine concerning purgatory …is a fond thing vainly invented and grounded upon no warranty of Scripture, but rather repugnant to the word of God'.

What then of my reservations about these two festivals? I have three to which I want to draw your attention.

No distinction between saints and souls

First, the distinction between saints and souls is not a biblical one. Until about 30 years ago children used to take an examination called the Eleven-plus. About 20% passed and went to a grammar school. For them the sky was the limit. They took GCE, often went on to university and in time occupied the top jobs in the professions, the civil service and industry. The 80% who failed the Eleven-plus often did not take GCE, they left school earlier, and they occupied the less prestigious, less glamorous and less well-paid jobs. In the 1960's we decided that we could not justify drawing that line at the age of eleven and so the Eleven-plus examination was phased out in most places and all children went to comprehensive schools. The sky was now the limit for everybody.

The Bible makes clear that for Christians too the sky is the limit for all. There are no grammar schools for saints and secondary modern schools for souls. We all go to comprehensive schools for saints. All Christians are saints, from the greatest to the least. It is not within the power of human beings to distinguish between people and assess their suitability for saint-hood. Of course there are people whose place in the life of faith is more prominent than others – St Paul, St Francis of Assisi, Mother Theresa, Desmond Tutu – but you and I are part of that great continuum.

But there is another distinction which I am uneasy about. We pray for 'those who have died in the faith of Christ' but sometimes we change the formula to include 'those whose faith is known to God alone.' This is a way of including people who no longer come to church, or who have lost the faith they once had. We want to give them the benefit of the doubt. No twenty-first century Christian can avoid recognising these if only because they are often members of our own family.

My brother-in-law was the son of an Anglican priest and himself an ordinand. He ceased to believe and when he died he was a Buddhist. His mother always wondered how she would explain to her husband when she met him in heaven that they would be joined by neither of their sons. One of the most outstanding boys I taught won a scholarship to Cambridge and was intending to be ordained. I was able to arrange what we would now call a gap year for him, teaching in Africa. The suffering he saw there destroyed his faith and made him an atheist. He became instead a teacher and has just retired after being a distinguished headmaster.

We all know people who for very honesty cannot believe; people whose experience of the church and Christian people has been a stumbling block; people for whom suffering, disease and disablement, their own or that of other people, makes belief in a God of love unthinkable. Then there are the people whose lives show love, compassion and practical goodness which put us to shame and yet who are not Christians. There are the people who in another age, another culture, and a different country would probably have been professing Christians. I want somehow to include them in the communion of saints. I was pleased to discover that the Lutheran church of USA includes people whom it regards as on the fringe of faith in its calendar, people like Michelangelo, Albrecht Durer, Copernicus and Dag Hammarschold.

No individual saints

My second reservation is that there are in the New Testament no individual saints. The Greek word for saint *agios*, is used no less than 65 times in the New Testament, mostly in Paul's letters and the book of Revelation but it is never used in the singular. It is always *agioi* – saints. There is in the New Testament no such thing as an individual saint. We are saints simply because we are members of the Christian community not because we are marked out by our goodness, or any individual act of sanctity. Some translations of the Bible have replaced the word saint by the phrase 'all God's people'.

So what we recall on All Saints' Day is individuals who are part of a great company which no man can number. That oneness of all Christian people is the emphasis of the great funeral hymn of Charles Wesley, one of his master-pieces:

> Come, let us join our friends above
> That have obtained the prize,
> And on the eagle wings of love
> To joys celestial rise.
> Let all the saints terrestrial sing
> With those to glory gone;
> For all the servants of our King,
> In earth and heaven, are one.
>
> One family we dwell in him
> Though now divided by the stream
> The narrow stream of death.[1]

To summarise so far: no distinction between saints and souls; no individual saints, only members of the household of God and finally saints are *not* espe-cially good.

Saints are not especially good

The word saint as we use it in normal speech conveys an unbiblical impres-sion. 'I'm no saint', we say with relief, meaning that we recognise our faults, don't lay claim to any virtues which might make us appear arrogant, and sometimes suggesting comparison with somebody who is rather sanctimo-nious. Or we say 'Of course he/she is a bit of a saint', meaning that they are unworldly, odd, have a screw loose and certainly not like us at all. Saints we assume should display all-round goodness. They find it easy to pray, never get angry, are not lustful, arrogant or selfish, go to church often and give generously to good causes.

You may remember Canon John Collins the campaigner for nuclear disarmament. After his death his widow Diana Collins wrote a memoir of him called *Partners in Protest*. She compared John, her husband with his fellow campaigner Michael Scott. 'John' she wrote 'was not a saint'. Michael Scott on the contrary was a saint, 'He was celibate, and didn't share John's liking for wine, cigars and gossip.' She was glad that she was not married to a saint!

Reviewing a life of Father Trevor Huddleston Dr Alan Wilkinson described him as one of the greatest Christians of the twentieth century, a man who made a whole generation proud to be an Anglican because of his courageous witness against apartheid in South Africa. But his biographer also describes Huddleston as susceptible to self-pity, a self- publicist, and intolerant of criticism. In other words he was both saint and sinner.

In fact of course an acquaintance with human nature makes us aware that we are all frail and flawed and if a saint has to display all round goodness there aren't any. And that applies to the heroes of the faith as well as to the run of the mill Christian. St Paul was boastful, intolerant, quick-tempered and he expected to get his own way. Martin Luther King was unfaithful to his wife. Dietrich Bonhoeffer took his friends to bull fights. Albert Schweitzer was a paternalist who treated native Africans like children. John Wesley made a disastrous marriage and was an autocrat.

Saints have feet of clay. No human has ever been nor ever will be able to demonstrate all round perfection. We are all on the way, all striving, but the sky's the limit.

I go to the National Portrait Gallery as often as I can. As you walk round the rooms you never know who you will meet next. The Queen and Margaret Thatcher are close to Robin Day, Bobby Charlton and Arthur Scargill. Princes and pop groups are next to each other. And so it is with the saints – freedom fighters and contemplative nuns, Indian peasants and Bible translators, prisoners of conscience and builders' labourers. It is like a Brueghel painting, a scene with soldiers and cripples, people making music, some fat, some ugly, all going about their daily work.

Today then we are, in the words of the book of Hebrews, 'surrounded by so great a cloud of witnesses' (12.1). Some of that great cloud lived in this town, worshipped in this church and are buried in the churchyard. Some are our ancestors remembered and forgotten who made us the people we are. Today we recall them with gratitude and love. That to me is the meaning of the communion of saints.

Let me finish with a quotation from Susan Hill's novel *In the Springtime of the Year*. It is about a young woman whose husband has died. At his funeral her feelings are described like this: 'what she became aware of was not the presence of the village people sitting or kneeling behind her but of others. The church was full of all those who had ever prayed in it, the air was crammed and vibrating with their goodness and the freedom and power of their resurrection. She felt herself to be part of some great living and growing tapestry'.

1. *Hymns and Psalms* Methodist Publishing House 1983 Number 812

DOCTRINES

Creeds

Every tongue should confess that Jesus Christ is Lord
Philippians 2.11

Bishop Hugh Montefiore said in the last book published before his recent death that 'the Church of England was the most credalised in all Christendom'. [1] At Morning and Evening Prayer we recite the Apostles Creed, at the Eucharist we say the Nicene Creed, when we baptise children or adults we rehearse the faith in a question and answer creed. *Common Worship* provides no less than seven alternative 'Affirmations of faith'. No other Christian church makes such extensive use of statements of faith in its regular worship.

All of which makes me uneasy. I have two problems with creeds. First, I find them difficult to understand and in places incomprehensible. The three creeds, which appear in the Prayer Book, were drawn up about 1600 years and they are very difficult for anybody to understand in the twenty first century. But second the Christian faith is a way of life and not chiefly assent to a set of intellectual propositions. Saying a creed is particularly unsuitable when there are many people in church who come only occasionally for example on Christmas Eve or for the Harvest Festival.

The ecumenical creeds of the church

Let me say something about each of the 'ecumenical' creeds, as they are called, creeds recognised by all Christian churches. There are three all with misleading names. The Apostles' Creed was not composed by the apostles, the Nicene Creed was not authorised by the Council of Nicea in 325 AD and the Athanasian Creed was not written by St Athanasius!

The earliest reference we have to the Apostles' Creed is in the eighth century though a similar statement of belief was used in a question and answer form at baptisms as early as the second century.

The Nicene Creed was intended to define the faith against heretics. In the early fourth century a priest from Alexandria named Arius denied that Jesus was really God so the so-called Nicene Creed was drawn up containing phrases which no follower of Arius could say conscientiously. It describes Jesus as ...'the only begotten Son of God, Begotten of his Father before all worlds, God of God, Light of Light, Very God of Very God, begotten not made, of one substance with the Father..' Well that didn't leave much to chance – and we are still reciting it 1600 years later.

The Athanasian Creed is even odder. It comes from Gaul in the fifth century. The Book of Common Prayer requires us to recite it on 13 specific occasions in the year but I have never heard it used in a church service. The reasons are not far to seek. It includes this remarkable verse: 'The Father incomprehensible, the Son incomprehensible: and the Holy Ghost incomprehensible'. But even worse it expresses twice, at the beginning and the end, this sentiment: ' Which faith except every one do keep whole and undefiled: without doubt he shall perish everlastingly'. From about the 1860s many church people experienced qualms about its continuing use and it ceased to be recited in services.

What are creeds for?

How then did the creeds arise in the early church? They served three purposes. First, they provided a summary of belief for anybody being baptised into the Christian faith, and took the form of question and answer. Then second, creeds served, as we have seen, to define the faith against heretics. Third, they were a battle cry, a marching song, a shout of triumph, a signature tune. They were rather like the *Red Flag, Land of Hope and Glory* or *We shall overcome*. They encouraged the faithful particularly in times of persecution.

But all those uses are questionable in the church today. We are no longer so concerned about heresy. We encourage people to think for themselves and to work out their faith over the years rather than accept a package which is unchangeable. It is hymns and worship songs which are more likely to constitute our marching song, or signature tune. The historic creeds are no longer a summary of what we are required to sign up to, a non-negotiable package.

But long before the church adopted formal creeds there were simple statements of what Christians believed. There are a number of these in the New Testament.

Creeds in the New Testament

The hymn 'At the name of Jesus', is based on what many people believe was the earliest creed, and it appears in the well known passage in the letter to the Philippians, simply 'Jesus Christ is Lord'. (Philippians 2.11). The same words are found in the First Letter to the Corinthians: 'No one can say Jesus is Lord except under the influence of the Holy Spirit.' (12.2), and in the

Letter to the Romans too: 'If you confess with your lips that Jesus is Lord and believe in your hearts that God raised him from the dead, you will be saved'. (10.9)

Some commentators say that even the gospels may have early creeds embedded in them. In answer to Jesus' question at Caesarea Philippi, 'Who do you say that I am?' Peter replies, 'You are the Messiah', which those who heard it would have recognised as a familiar affirmation of faith.

In the Acts of the Apostles there is the story of the meeting between Philip and the Ethiopian court official on the Wilderness road between Jerusalem and Gaza. Philip preaches the gospel to him and he asks if he can be baptised. Philip replies 'If you believe with all your heart, you may [be baptised]', and he replies 'I believe that Jesus is the Son of God'. (8.37)[2]

Some creeds found in the New Testament are longer and more developed. This one for example from the First Letter to the Corinthians 'There is one God and one Lord Jesus Christ through whom are all things and through whom we exist' (8.6). And another one in one of the last books of the New Testament to be written, the First Letter to Timothy –'He was revealed in flesh, vindicated in spirit, seen by angels, proclaimed among Gentiles, believed in throughout the world, taken up in glory' (3.16).

What does it mean to say Jesus is Lord?

If the earliest Christian creed was 'Jesus is Lord' what would it mean for us to make a similar affirmation? Let me give you two illustrations. Towards the end of his very long life the veteran socialist Fenner Brockway reminisced in a BBC documentary about his experiences as a journalist in the early years of the twentieth century. He was once sent to interview Keir Hardie, one of the very first working class MPs, elected for West Ham South in 1892. Fenner Brockway was profoundly impressed by Keir Hardie. 'I cannot convey the depth of his ringing Scottish accents as he declared his faith. I went to hear him a young Liberal, I left him a young socialist'. Those baptismal converts in the early church had a similar experience. They expressed their new found faith in the words 'Jesus is Lord'. They were captivated by him, his words, his personality, his risen presence. That perhaps catches something of the appeal and fascination of what we may feel for Jesus.

Colin Morris is a Methodist minister who made his name in Zambia, was later President of the Methodist Conference and later still head of Religious Broadcasting. He is an outstanding preacher, writer and broadcaster with a remarkable knack of presenting religious truth powerfully and memorably. His faith has been expressed mostly through social and political action. He has probably never preached a devotional sermon in his life and the last word you could apply to him is pious. He was once interviewed by a religious affairs correspondent who asked him, 'Has Christianity done anything for you as a person inside? Does it affect you as a man?' Colin Morris replied, ' I know that within me are forces which are strong enough to destroy me and I believe that Jesus Christ has prevented that self-destruction. I believe I would have destroyed myself had it not been for him'. He could have added 'So he is my Lord and saviour'. That too perhaps expresses something of what Christian commitment can mean to us.

'Jesus is Lord' – a statement which many of us would be reticent about making or even embarrassed to speak out loud. But it is the heart of the creed. It is a description of the key place Jesus plays in the life of any Christian. It is he who saves us from ourselves, who helps us to make sense of life, determines our values and influences our relationships.

The belief of the church

The first creeds were then very simple. They arose from experience and described the new life which converts were living as a result of their encounter with Jesus. Only later were the historic creeds of the church introduced. I believe that we should start where the first Christians did. I'm glad that the Nicene Creed, unlike the Apostles' Creed, begins not 'I believe', but 'We believe'. Creeds summarise what the church believes or if you prefer, what there is to be believed, what's on offer, what I can explore in the course of a lifetime. We do not have to sign up to each item of the creeds. Some beliefs are more important than others; some are expressed in language which is out of date, some I have mental reservations about. A creed should not be a strait jacket constraining me to affirm what I do not believe. It is much more like a marching song, a shout of triumph, a signature tune.

1. Hugh Montefiore *Looking afresh* SPCK 2002 p.1
2. NRSV omits verse Acts 8.37 but adds in a footnote: 'Other ancient authorities add all or most of verse 37'.

What is humanity?

*What are human beings that you are mindful of them,
mortals that you care for them?* Psalm 8.4-5

William Golding was one of the great writers of the twentieth century. *Lord
of the flies,* the novel which made his name, was published in 1954. A plane
carrying English schoolboys crash-lands on a coral island and all the adults
are missing. The island is reminiscent of R.M.Ballantyne's *Coral Island*
(published almost a century before in 1857). All should be well. They are
nice, well brought up boys from suburbia. But almost at once things begin
to go wrong. There is a struggle for leadership. Ralph is elected leader and
so Jack the unsuccessful candidate leads his followers to another part of the
island determined to capture the conch shell which is the agreed symbol of
authority. Then there is the failure through jealousy and idleness to keep
alight the fire, which might attract a nearby ship or a passing aircraft and so
bring release. There is the scorn and intolerance of the short, fat, asthmatic
boy whom they cruelly nickname Piggy whose spectacles are broken in a
fight leaving him half blind. The story culminates in the death of two boys,
Simon and Piggy and the island is left a burning ruin. At the end a British
naval officer appears.

> The officer inspected the little scarecrow in front of him. The kid needed a
> bath, a haircut, a nose wipe and a good deal of ointment. 'Nobody killed, I
> hope...' 'Only two.' The officer leaned down and looked closely at Ralph.
> 'Two? Killed?' Ralph nodded. Behind him the whole island was shud-
> dering with flame. 'I should have thought', said the officer, 'that a pack of
> British boys – you are all British aren't you? – would have been able to put
> up a better show than that' ... Ralph looked at him dumbly. For a moment
> he had a fleeting picture of the strange glamour that had once invested the
> beaches. But the island was scorched up like dead wood. ... The tears
> began to flow and the sobs shook him.... Ralph wept for the end of inno-
> cence, the darkness of man's heart. [1]

In *Lord of the flies* William Golding wrote a modern parable, a parable of the
human situation, the enigma of humanity, the tragedy of the world. Yet we
scarcely need a parable to remind us of the dark side of human nature. Every
newspaper and television news bulletin brings corroboration.

I want this morning to speak about human nature as God sees it and as
the Bible reveals it. I want us to think not about humanity at its worst or at

its best, not human beings in the abstract, not the other person but about you and me and our neighbours.

I want to make four points. We are first of all creatures made for lordship.

Creatures made for lordship

The early chapters of Genesis make clear that we have much in common with animals. We are born as they are and die as they do; we breathe and eat as they do. We are, in the famous phrase of Desmond Morris, 'Naked apes'. But we are also different from animals. We can walk upright, we have movable thumbs, and larger brains and we can make fire. We are creatures who have memories and self-awareness. Our sexuality is not just physiological but it can be the bearer of relationships of love and self-sacrifice. We were made for lordship over the earth. We can make it a dustbowl or a fertile countryside. We can harness nuclear power to bring untold destruction or to cure cancer. We can lay mines to kill and maim. We can abuse animals in circuses and broiler houses or use them to cultivate the soil and for companionship. That's you and me – human beings made by God for Lordship over his world; it's our inescapable responsibility.

Sinful creatures

Second we are sinful creatures. The Greek word translated sin, *hamartia*, can also mean 'falling short of the mark', perhaps a better translation for those for whom the word sin has been overused or blunted by familiarity. John Howe, the seventeenth century Puritan once said 'Man is a stately ruin bearing the doleful inscription, 'Here God once dwelt''. There is in human beings both individually and collectively a massive disorder, a fundamental distortion, which prevents us fulfilling our God given potential. We are made to control nature, the world and the universe but we cannot control ourselves. Given a rich, productive world we have turned it into a place where one third starve, one third are undernourished and one third consume four fifths of the world's goods with a prodigality which would be incredible if it were not a well-observed fact. We are being warned that we could be on the verge of destroying the future viability of the earth altogether.

Desmond Morris says 'The sombre fact is that we are the cruellest, most ruthless species that has ever walked the earth', and the history of the twentieth century provided overwhelming corroboration of his judgement. Sin, missing the mark, whether it takes the form of mass murder, greed, lust, or bullying carried out by school children to the point where they can drive the victim to suicide, is simply a feature of human beings. We are sinful creatures.

Responsible creatures

There is a saying of G.K.Chesterton; 'If I wish to dissuade a man from drinking his tenth whisky and soda, I slap him on the back and say, 'Be a man'. No one who wished to dissuade a crocodile from eating its tenth explorer would slap it on the back and say, 'Be a crocodile''. That witticism enshrines an important truth. Men and women and children too are accountable. We can decide how we wish to behave. If you played football badly yesterday you can say to yourself, 'This won't do, I must try harder, I need more training'.

We are responsible – or are we? A boy steals and ends up in court. And the neighbours say 'Well what can you expect with a father like that and a brother already in gaol' – heredity is to blame it appears. Or they may say, 'What can you expect with friends like that' – it's all the fault of the environment in which they have been brought up. 'Ah well you can't change human nature'. People blame heredity, environment, psychological factors. Determinism is so often our let-out. After a period in prison a high proportion of those released reoffend and often return to prison. And of course the determinists are partly right. Psychology reveals the limits within which we are free. And yet in the last resort we have a curious feeling that he or she needn't have done it. The conviction that we are free to make choices remains deeply within us. We talk about people rising above themselves or we say 'You'd never have thought she had it in her'. When all the excuses are made we are free agents – our consciences can be reached, we are accountable for ourselves, God can address us.

Creatures made for lordship, sinful creatures, responsible creatures and finally redeemable creatures.

Redeemable creatures

The author of the text of Handel's *The Messiah* began with the aria *Comfort ye my people*. He followed that with *Every valley shall be exalted* and then the chorus '*And the glory of the Lord shall be revealed*, because the Christian faith is a gospel of salvation, it is good news.

Running right through the Bible, from Moses to the prophets and on into the New Testament is the hope of salvation. Human beings can be saved from sin, self-centredness and pride and can be restored to a right relationship with the God who made them. To St Paul salvation goes beyond individual human beings. It includes the whole human situation and even the universe itself. 'The creation itself', he writes 'will be set free from its bondage to decay and will obtain the freedom of the glory of the children of God' (Romans 8.21).

A doctrine of humanity is as important for Christians as a doctrine of God. But it is more than just a theoretical doctrine. It has to become a guide to action. Who we are is the key to how we behave to ourselves, to our fellow human beings and to the universe in which God has placed us. We recognise in ourselves the pride, envy, and selfishness which spoil us. In our dealings with other people we remember that they are made by God, never to be treated as less than his people. In our approach to the world in which we live we recall that we share responsibility for the use of its rich resources. In our attitude to even the worst in our society – murderers and paedophiles for example – however hard it may be, we acknowledge that they are addressable and redeemable by the grace of God.

The film version of *Lord of the flies* has running through it the haunting refrain of the *Kyrie eleison,* Lord have mercy. That is perhaps the final word which we utter in recognition of our human situation.

1   William Golding *Lord of the flies* Penguin edition 1960 pp191–92

Justification by faith

Since we are justified by faith we have peace with God through our Lord Jesus Christ. Romans 5.1

Martin Luther was probably the most influential Christian between St Francis of Assisi in the thirteenth century and John Wesley in the eighteenth century. He was the son of a copper miner in Saxony. He studied at the university of Erfurt and became an Augustinian friar. He was serious minded and in deadly earnest about his Christian faith. He had a sensitive conscience and a sense of sin which was almost pathological. He wrote:

> I tried as hard as I could to keep the Rule. I used to be contrite and make a list of my sins. I confessed them again and again. I carried out the penances allotted to me. And yet my conscience kept nagging me: it kept telling me 'You fell short there; you left that sin off your list; you were not sorry

enough.' The more I tried these human remedies the more troubled and uneasy my conscience grew.

He studied St Paul and particularly the letter to the Romans and came to accept the impact of Paul's words *The just shall live by faith* (1.17 AV). He realised that he could never be saved by his own efforts. He could never say enough prayers, never fast sufficiently nor do enough good works to get right with God. There was nothing he could do for God; he could only accept what God had done for him. And so he rediscovered in his own experience the Pauline doctrine of justification by faith, the theme particularly of the letters to the Galatians and Romans. It had been overlaid by the complex sacramental system of the middle ages, as it was later to be neglected once more by the rational churchmen of the eighteenth century.

That doctrine was the power behind the sixteenth century Reformation as later to be the dynamic of the eighteenth century evangelical revival. It is central to the Thirty Nine Articles of the Church of England. Article II entitled Of the Justification of Man reads: 'We are accounted righteous before God, only for the merits of our Lord and Saviour Jesus Christ by Faith, and not for our own works or deservings; Wherefore that we are justified by Faith only is a most wholesome Doctrine and very full of comfort'...

What is justification by faith?

Quite simply justification by faith is the teaching that God accepts us as righteous even though he knows that we are no such thing. He treats us as good people even though we are not. He restores our lost standing with him even though we don't deserve it. We can do nothing to deserve God's favour, his love or his grace – nothing that is except have faith in Christ. It represents the paradox that the harder you try to please God the less likely you are to succeed.

Let me give you a human analogy. A businessman who has been in prison for corrupt business dealings is released and returns to his respectable suburban home. How will his neighbours treat him? They can either treat him as he deserves – put him on probation before he is invited to the bridge parties, allowed to rejoin the golf club or become again a member of Rotary or they can accept him unconditionally, without any reserve, give him back his lost status in the community. Which is more likely to achieve his rehabilitation? Only the second is likely to work. A period of ostracism is the quickest route back to gaol. He has to be treated as someone he isn't in order to stand the slightest chance of going straight and becoming the person he may now resolve to become. There is a similar dynamic in being treated by God as the people we ought to be rather than the people we are. It is the same in school – a pupil told repeatedly that he or she is stupid, idle and good for nothing soon lives up to expectation; what I used to describe as the 4C syndrome. Pupils have to be treated instead as the people we hope they may become.

Two objections

There are two objections which are sometimes advanced to the doctrine of justification by faith.

First, doesn't it cheapen salvation? People don't value what they don't pay for: a salvation which is free is valueless. Doesn't it discourage good works? Why bother to go to church, receive Holy Communion, say our prayers, give to good causes or devote our time to serving other people? Shouldn't we just go on sinning in order to give God more to forgive? Paul anticipates just such an argument in the letter to the Romans 'Should we continue in sin in order that grace may abound?' and then replies to his own question: 'By no means! How can we who died to sin go on living in it?'(6.1–2)

Or to put it another way: Doesn't God rate at all a life devoted to his service? There is a profound theological answer to that. The Christian gospel is one of grace – God's undeserved favour poured out on us. Our response is Christian behaviour, worship, prayer and sacrament – our service is not in order to deserve God's favour but to express our gratitude to him. When we come to church, read the Bible, say our prayers or serve God in daily life we do it not to earn salvation but to show our gratitude. Our motive is not duty but thankfulness. That too has a human parallel. When we care for aged parents or our sometimes erring children we do it not out of duty or to earn their approval but out of gratitude and love. Isaac Watts puts it in a memorable couplet: 'Love so amazing, so divine,/ Demands my soul, my life, my all.'

Second, isn't salvation by faith the teaching of Paul not Jesus? Some people have argued that Paul added theological complexity to the simple message of Jesus or even that he distorted it. It is true that you will not find the word justification outside Paul's letters; it scarcely passes the lips of Jesus. I believe however that Jesus did teach justification by faith but he did as he did everything else by means of stories or parables.

The parable of the Prodigal Son (Luke 15.22-24) is pure justification by faith. The Prodigal rehearses how he will justify himself – 'I have sinned...I am not worthy to be called your son ... make me a hired servant'. But he is never allowed to finish his catalogue of self justification before his father says 'Bring the best robe... put a ring on his finger and shoes on his feet .. Kill the fatted calf'. He is not treated as the waster, the good for nothing which he is but as his father's son who has come home. And not surprisingly the elder son finds that hard to take. Pure justification by faith!

The story of the Pharisee and the Publican (Luke 18.9-14) contains the same message. The Pharisee prides himself on not being a thief, a rogue, an adulterer or even like 'this tax collector'. Instead he fasts twice a week and gives a tenth of all his income. All the tax collector can say is, 'God be merciful to me a sinner'. And Jesus says: 'I tell you that man went down to his house justified rather than the other'(18.14). Once more pure justification by faith and incidentally the only time Jesus is recorded using the word justified in its Pauline sense.

The eighteenth century hymn writer Thomas Toplady puts it like this in his well known hymn *Rock of Ages*: 'Not the labour of my hands / can fulfil thy law's demands; /could my zeal no respite know, / could my tears for ever flow, / all for sin could not atone:/ thou must save, and thou alone'.

Peace with God

Let me return finally to the text from Romans chapter 5. 'As we are justified by faith, then let us enjoy the peace we have with God through our Lord Jesus Christ' (verse 1, Moffat's translation.) For Paul peace meant no longer striving to fulfil all the demands of the Jewish law. For Luther it meant escaping from the wrath of God and his own failure to live up to the requirements of his monastic order. For us peace is expressed rather differently. It means acceptance of ourselves as we are, awareness that we are no longer at cross-purposes with God. It means an inward peace of mind, acceptance that we are psychologically content and at ease with the world in which our lot has fallen.

And all that is the fruit of this central doctrine of the Christian faith. It is a doctrine we associate with the Reformation and with Martin Luther. It is however the catholic doctrine which lies at the heart of the gospel, a Biblical doctrine, rediscovered in the sixteenth century and again in the eighteenth century and central to our faith in the twenty first century. 'Let us enjoy the peace we have with God through our Lord Jesus Christ.'

Church – divine or human?

You are a chosen race, a royal priesthood, a dedicated nation,
a people claimed by God for his own, to proclaim the triumphs
of him who called you out of darkness into his marvellous light.
1 Peter 2. 9-10

In about an hour's time and after a cup of coffee most of us will sit down to attend the annual parish meeting. We shall receive reports about the activities of the church during the year – from the Mothers' Union, Sunday Club, Friends of St Peter's, Parish News, the Church Overseas Support Team and so on. We shall hear about the state of our finances and about plans for the permanent dais for the nave altar and for the proposed coffee area under the gallery. We shall elect churchwardens, sidespersons and PCC members. In fact it will be just like the AGM of any other organisation of which we may be members – golf club, parents association, Parish Council or local history society. So what differentiates the church from these organisations or does anything? What sort of organisation is the church? Here are two contrasting pictures.

The New Testament picture

The first picture of the church is derived from our foundation document, the New Testament. One of the best-known descriptions of the church comes from the First Letter of Peter. The writer is addressing the gentile churches in Asia Minor. They are having a rough time, they are scorned and victimised by their fellow citizens. So the writer seeks to improve their morale and raise their self-esteem. He describes them in imagery drawn from the Old Testament. 'You are a chosen race' – just like the Jews; 'You are a royal priesthood' – like the priesthood of the Old Testament; 'You are a dedicated nation'; 'You are a people claimed by God for his own'.

But that is not the only place in the New Testament where the church is described in high-flown language. The best-known metaphor of all is that used in the first letter to the Corinthians and in Ephesians and Colossians: 'You are the body of Christ'. Elsewhere in Ephesians the writer says 'Christ loved the church and gave himself for it'. (5.25). When the New Testament uses the word *ekklesia* it sometimes means the local church, sometimes the universal church and sometimes the mystical church but in each case the church is a divine society, it has been called by God and given a mission by him.

And that imagery is picked up in our hymns and by our theologians. As the hymn *The Church's one Foundation* claims: 'She is his new creation .../ From heaven he came and sought her/ To be his holy bride/ With his own blood he bought her / And for her life he died'. The theologian John Macquarrie, refers with approval to the description of the church as 'the extension of the incarnation', the body through which Christ is represented on earth.[1]

To all of which we reply – what us, St Peter's Bishop's Waltham, the Church of England – the body of Christ, a royal priesthood, a holy temple, bride of Christ, a chosen race, the extension of the incarnation? You must be joking.

The sociologist's picture

The second picture of the church is that of the dispassionate outsider, of neighbours who do not go to church or the sociologist. To the sociologist the church is an in-group existing for the sake of its own members. As the countryman said to his neighbour who was a churchwarden, 'Your hobby's church, mine's pigs', or as his wife might have said, 'Your fix is the Mothers' Union, mine's the Women's Institute.' To the sociologist the church is just like other secular societies: it rises and declines, over time it may become rigid, reactionary, resistant to change, exclusive and self-centred. We could I am sure all make a list of the very human ways in which the church behaves, ways we have come to take for granted: its arcane debates about doctrine, its obsession in recent years with liturgical change, its bizarre hierarchy of Right Reverends, Very Reverends and Venerables, the irrelevance of much of its life and above all its disunity. I've just read a book by Monica Furlong called *C.of E: the state it's in*. It is written with much affection and profound knowledge of the Church of England but it is nonetheless a sobering read.

Divine society or human society?

Well which is it – the Body of Christ, a divine society or the sociologist's church, an all too human society? The answer of course is not either/or but both/and. The church is both a royal priesthood, the body of Christ; a divine society which has outlasted every other human organisation perhaps the only institution which has existed for nearly 2000 years and spread right across the world. But it is also a fallible organisation consisting of sinful mortals like you and me, implicated all too obviously in the ways of the world.

How then shall we reconcile the two? Let me draw a parallel. Some of us will remember the shock we experienced when House of Commons debates were first broadcast and then televised. Question time reminded us of disorderly schoolboys baiting a vulnerable teacher. Even now the Speaker sometimes sounds more like a football referee than Speaker of the mother of parliaments. Debates often take place in an almost empty Chamber. Members spend a great deal of time in scoring points off each other. How ludicrous – can there really be any future in such an organisation? But beneath the triviality, the childish behaviour, the outdated rituals is something of infinite worth. The House of Commons enshrines democracy, safeguards freedom of speech and freedom of the press, guarantees equality before the law.

So it is with the church. It is subject to sin, corruption, division, irrelevance, and triviality, and it is so easy to make fun of it and even to write it off. But it embodies the gospel of Jesus Christ, the message of the love of God, the primacy of faith, hope and love. It enshrines the truth of Jesus who heals and frees. However corrupt it may seem there is always the possibility of new life; it is *semper reformanda,* always capable of being reformed. The church is both/and, both human and divine. And what is true of the universal church is true too of St Peter's. Our AGM is a business meeting but the business is part of God's business in this place.

Two conditions for the church of God

Let me finish by suggesting two conditions the church must fulfil if it is indeed to be God's church, the divine society and not just another human organisation, the sociologist's in-group.

First, it must include all Christians. No Christian communion can claim to be the true church not Roman Catholic, nor Orthodox, nor Methodist not even the Church of England. None can claim to have the only valid sacraments, the only real priesthood, or a monopoly of faith or holiness. Even if we made little progress in the twentieth century towards organic unity at least at grass roots level we have stopped unchurching each other. Sadly of course we have to acknowledge that this is not wholly true even now. In our own diocese there is the unlovely sight of churches which will not accept the sacramental ministry of our diocesan bishop because he is prepared to ordain women. But as soon as we equate the Body of Christ with our own denomination or our own point of view we are in trouble. The church of all Christians is God's church; the church of denominations is the sociologist's church.

Second, it must be available for all people. We all know William Temple's aphorism that the church is the only organisation which exists for the sake of those who are not its members. It is of course like all generalisations only partly true. But the truth it enshrines is of vital importance. The church is not just for those who attend its services, contribute to its upkeep or accept its teaching. We are a servant church. We are here for the uncommitted, the unconverted, the doubter, the occasional attender, for those who want a nice back drop for their wedding photograph, a dignified departure from this life or to mark the birth of a child by bringing him or her for baptism. And it is for those in need who have nowhere else to turn. In the forecourt of Wesley's Chapel, London, the mother church of Methodism, is a statue of John Wesley on horseback with a Bible in his hand. It is facing outwards on to City Road, not inwards towards the chapel.

We would all agree in principle that the church is for all people. The problem is in putting this into practice. Suppose we need to move time honoured pews to make a social area, or change the time of services to welcome those who cannot come otherwise or recognise the calls made on the Rector's time by the village rather than the church and by those who do not contribute to the Parish Share. Suppose we are taken for a ride by rogues and scroungers. Can we still retain our vision that we exist for all people? A church for all people is God's church; a church which exists only for its own members is the sociologists's church.

So this morning as we hold our annual parochial meeting we remember our two-fold nature. We are a human society. The church consists of ordinary men, women and children like you and me – sinful, fallible, selfish, short-sighted but also well intentioned, compassionate, and sometimes loving, and unselfish. We are also a divine society, part of the Body of Christ, called into a worldwide fellowship, transcending race, colour, gender, nationality. And the true church is for all Christians and for all people.

1. John Macquarrie *Principles of Christian theology* SCM 1977 p.389

Priesthood

The priesthood which Jesus holds is perpetual. Hebrews 7.24
You are a royal priesthood. 1 Peter 2.9

Almost 15 months ago the PCC met to agree the Parish Profile, for submission to the Lord Chancellor's patronage secretary. The last section was a description of the sort of parish priest we were looking for.[1]

Our identikit rector should be between 35 and 40, married with 2.4 children. This should be neither his first incumbency nor his last – we want somebody neither inexperienced nor worn out. He should be a good visitor, administrator, teacher, preacher and chairman but able to delegate. He should be good with the Tiny Tots, adolescents and the elderly and of course with those of us who do not fall into any of these categories. In theology he should be neither too radical nor too conservative; in churchmanship neither too catholic nor too evangelical but of course a man of definite convictions. His personal qualities should include tact, humour and patience and he should exemplify the theological virtues of faith, hope and love. The Archdeacon pointed out to us that we were not likely to get our identikit rector – he himself already had a job and the Archangel Gabriel was not available either. Now I am of course guilty of preacher's exaggeration, but you get the point I am making.

What then are our legitimate expectations of our new parish priest as he begins his ministry here next week and, at least as important, what can he expect from us?

Priesthood in the New Testament

Let me start with priesthood in the New Testament. Only two books in the New Testament refer to Christian priesthood and in neither case is it to a parish priest in our sense. Jesus is described no less than 28 times in the book of Hebrews as our High Priest. It is Jesus who has experienced what it is to be human and can therefore be the bridge-builder (the literal meaning of priest) between sinful man and holy God. It is through him that we offer prayer; it is he who understands our infirmities because he has lived a human life. His is the fundamental priesthood.

But secondly the First Epistle of Peter talks about the whole church community as a 'chosen race, a royal priesthood, a holy nation, a people called by God for his own possession'. Notice it is the whole church which is described as a priesthood, not individual Christians. It is the whole Christian community which is called to share Christ's priesthood, to be bridge-builders, to hold the world before God.

Priesthood in church history

How then you may ask did the word priest come to be attached to the ordained ministry? The New Testament words for minister include deacon, pastor, presbyter and elder but never priest. It was not until the third century in *The Apostolic Tradition* of Hippolytus about 215AD that the

ordination prayer for a bishop names him high priest and even later before
the word priest is used of a presbyter. So the emphasis shifts from the priesthood of Christ entrusted to the whole people of God to the priesthood of
an ordained clergy. The result is a distortion of New Testament teaching,
and it leads in the Middle Ages to a passive people and a dominant priesthood. The Eucharist for example ceases to be the action of the whole people
and becomes instead an action performed by the priest on behalf of the
people who become spectators. (Incidentally we have returned to the earlier
practice – we no longer speak of the priest as the celebrant. Instead he is the
president and it is we the whole people who do the celebrating.) It is for
that reason that the churches of the Reformation rejected the word priest
for ordained clergy and used instead the words minister or pastor. They
emphasised the priesthood of all believers though they individualised it and
each believer was seen as a priest.

To sum up: in the New Testament the priesthood was Christ's, conferred
by him on the whole Christian community. Both catholics and protestants
distorted the New Testament idea of priesthood: the catholic tradition
emphasised the individual ordained priest, whilst protestants emphasised
the individual Christian. In the last 50 years we have recovered a New
Testament emphasis. Christ confers his priesthood on the whole church but
in a twofold form: there is a priesthood of the ordained and a priesthood of
the baptised. They are complementary; the one exists to activate and facilitate the other. As we welcome our new parish priest I want to say a little
about his priesthood and about ours.

The priesthood of the ordained

We live in the day of the job description. The job description of the
ordained priest is set out in the ordination service and ought in my view to
be much better known than it is. Here is an extract.

> He is to proclaim the word of the Lord, to call his hearers to repentance,
> and in Christ's name to absolve, and to declare the forgiveness of sins. He
> is to baptize, and prepare the baptized for Confirmation. He is to preside
> at the celebration of Holy Communion. He is to lead his people in prayer
> and worship, to intercede for them, to bless them in the name of the Lord,
> and to teach and encourage by word and example. He is to minister to the
> sick, and prepare the dying for their death.....

Then these words are addressed to the men and women to be ordained
priest:

You are to be messengers, watchmen and stewards of the Lord; you are to teach and to admonish, to feed and to provide for the Lord's family, to search for his children in the wilderness of this world's temptations and to guide them through its confusions, so that they may be saved through Christ for ever.[1]

So the rector has a discipline of prayer and Bible reading; he has a ministry of word and sacrament, of blessing and absolution. He presides at the Eucharist. He has a ministry to the sick and dying. But more important than the individual items of the job is the priestly character which it illuminates. When we have a curate he or she is at first a deacon and the most important part of the training is what is called ' priestly formation'; the deacon is learning in the parish the discipline which enables him or her to live the life of an ordained priest amidst all the pressures of daily life. So much for the priesthood of the ordained minister. Let me turn to our priesthood, the priesthood of the baptised.

The priesthood of the baptised

Baptism is nothing less than admission to the priesthood of God's people but there is no job description for the priesthood of the baptised. Let me however say three things about our priesthood.

First, we must be prepared *to complement* the rector's ministry. His priesthood can only be complete when we share it and when he exemplifies and articulates the priesthood of the whole Christian community.

Worship is not his alone. He presides but it is we, the whole people who celebrate. We lead the ministry of the word, read lessons, lead prayers, administer the chalice, share the Peace, not to relieve the monotony of one voice or because there are not enough ordained priests but to express the priesthood of the whole people.

Pastoral care is not his alone. We share in baptismal preparation, bereavement counselling, visit the sick, take communion to the house-bound, welcome newcomers – as part of the priesthood of the whole church. The ordained priest is our leader, he trains and guides but it is one of the unexpected bonuses of a shortage of clergy that we have had to return to the New Testament doctrine of the whole people of God.

Prayer is not his alone either. I am sorry that it is so often an ordained person who is asked to pray on a public occasion, to say Grace or to open the PCC with prayer. Prayer is part of the work of the priesthood of the baptised.

Second, we must *facilitate* his ministry. Some churches have their own unwritten job description for the rector and it doesn't bear much relation to the job description in the ordination service. If the lawn mower needs repair, or the parish magazine has to be duplicated, or the Christmas tree has to be decorated then it is the rector who is expected to do it. After all he has plenty of time while we are busy lay people. Now I do not despise any of these jobs; they are all part of an incarnational church and the rector will no doubt help. But it is not here that the heart of his ministry lies: that is spelt out in the ordination service.

Nor do his duties end with the churches and communities of which he is parish priest. He represents us in the wider church: he has responsibilities to the deanery and the diocese, to Churches Together, to his fellow clergy and to the Church of England as a whole. He needs time to read and think, to go on retreat so that he can share his vision with us. We have to enable him to do these things not regard them as an unwelcome distraction from his care for us.

Then we must give him time to be human – to watch television and read books, pursue secular interests, go on holiday, enjoy a private life, meet sinners as well as saints. We must respect and insist that he takes his day off.

Finally, we must be prepared *to share his failure* with him. By failure I do not just mean that he will not measure up to our unrealistic expectations, that he will have failings like all of us, not be equally good at all aspects of his ministry, and won't please all of us all the time. Nor do I mean that he will not live up to his own hopes and expectations – which of us does?

What I mean is something much deeper. He will have to reckon with the fact that at one level the church is a failure. In the west decline has now lasted for well over a century. To most people living in Bishop's Waltham, as to people living elsewhere in Great Britain and much of western Europe, the gospel is seen as an irrelevance. The rector will meet much goodwill but alongside that he will also encounter indifference or even hostility to what he stands for. As many of us know from our own families the younger generation is largely unchurched. Many of the young people who are confirmed do not enter actively into church life; they regard confirmation as permission to stop coming to church. The rector has to live with that burden and we must share his inevitable sense of failure. But then the gospel is about failure, Christ ended up on a Cross before he was raised.

On Friday we shall meet for the institution and induction of our new rector. And next Sunday we shall welcome him to preside at the Eucharist for the first time as our parish priest. They will be joyful occasions. They will be moments of dedication for him and for us. They will be opportunities to remind ourselves that Christ confers his priesthood on the whole church and that the rector as an ordained priest and we as people baptised into the priesthood of the whole church each have our part to play in its ministry.

1   A sermon preached at Parish Communion the Sunday before the institution of the new Rector. I used extracts from the ordination service in the *Alternative Service Book 1980* pp.356-357 because the *Common Worship* ordination service had not then been authorised.

ɕ

Laity

If I asked you what you understand by the word laity you would probably reply in negative terms. Laity you would say describes people who are *not* clergy; they constitute the rank and file of the church; they occupy the pews rather than the stall, the pulpit or the altar. Or you might say laity are *not* expert, they are amateurs. You would not expect them to know about the Lambeth Quadrilateral or who the Monophysites were. You might add that laity are *not* full-time members of the church – they come on Sundays when they can; they rush in to the PCC meeting after a busy day at the office, a hastily snatched supper or after putting the children to bed. And of course laity are un-paid.

Now I am a member of the laity – and so are you! So we are amateur, part-time, unpaid, non-clerical Christians; sheep in the flock of the clerical shepherd. You will not be surprised to hear that it is a definition with which I am far from satisfied. I want this morning to talk about what it is to be a lay Christian.

A theology of laity

The Biblical basis of laity is twofold, deriving from two words which together constitute a theology of the laity. In Greek the words are *laos*, meaning people and *cosmos* meaning world.

Laos. God's choice of a people is one of the great themes of the Bible. In the Old Testament God chooses the Jews to be his people. He makes a covenant with them and through thick and thin he remains faithful to them and they remain his people. In the New Testament St Paul speaks of the gentiles joining the Jews as the new people of God, the church.

To be laity is then to be simply part of the people of God, something we become by baptism. And the *laos* of God includes the clergy. So we are all part of the people of God. The English word laity and the Greek word *laos* have different meanings. Laity is negative and exclusive, *laos* is positive and inclusive.

In the Middle Ages the clergy hijacked the church and from then on there were two classes of people; clergy – those in parishes, cathedrals and monasteries – who were the active part of the church and the laity who were passive. At the Reformation Luther and Calvin tried to get rid of the distinction, emphasising the calling of the laity but they were only partially successful; hints of it remain to this day.

Cosmos. The second word essential to the calling of the people of God is *cosmos*, the Greek word for world. We are called to serve God in his world. Genesis chapter one ends: 'God saw everything that he had made and indeed it was very good.' (Genesis 1.31) In the Lord's Prayer we pray 'Your will be done on earth' (Matthew 6.10). One of the best-known verses in the Bible is John 3.16. It begins 'God so loved the world'. We often forget that part of the sentence because we concentrate on the second part. The Greek word for world is *cosmos*. So the world of nature and human relations, the world of work and leisure, politics and business, art and entertainment, music and culture are all owned by God. So the people of God are called not out of the world but into the world God loved and loves. So the theological basis for our membership of the laity is summed up in those two words *laos* and *cosmos*.

Clergy and laity

How then do we differentiate the roles of clergy and laity in the church? Some time ago the rector spoke at a family service about the distinctive job of the parish priest. In a service he said there are three things which only an ordained priest can do and they are easily remembered because they begin with A, B and C. A priest Absolves, Blesses and Consecrates. As a Reader I cannot do these things. If I take a service I use a different form of words in the absolution. When children come to the communion rail I say *May the Lord bless you*, whereas a priest will omit the word *May*. And of course I cannot consecrate the elements at Holy Communion.

But that is all. All the other things which the church does are shared tasks. Anything else not only can a lay person do but he or she should do because it is part of the task of the whole people of God. We are all pastors, all evangelists, all teachers. That doesn't mean that some people aren't better at some of these tasks than others – Paul knew that perfectly well.

But it is hard to practise because we are used to a clerically dominated church. It can suit both parties. Some clergy prefer a deskilled, subservient laity and some lay people regard it as a blessed release if the clergy take all the decisions.

One of the few advantages of the decline in the number of clergy is that laity are less able to rely on full time priests to do everything for them. We have to be more active. We have learnt in recent years not to regard a Reader taking a service or preaching as a regrettable necessity but as a valuable resource. People increasingly recognise that a visit to somebody sick in hospital, hospice or at home undertaken by a lay person is just as much a church visit as one undertaken by a priest. And acceptance of Readers taking funerals has grown steadily. It is half a century since Mark Gibbs a very active Anglican layman wrote a book about the laity called *God's Frozen People* but since then the ice has slowly melted and is likely to go on doing so.

Increasingly we recognise that it is not chiefly the laity's job to help the priest run the church but the priest's job to equip the lay people to be the church in the world.

Monday to Saturday ministries

So far I have spoken mostly about what have been called 'Sunday ministries', laity active in the domestic life of the church, as churchwardens, sidespersons, Readers, intercessors, house group leaders, PCC members, acolytes and servers amongst other things. More important are 'Monday ministries', the responsibility of Christians in the structures of industry, commerce, politics and the professions, at work in office, shop or petrol station. More recently still we have recognised the role of Christians in what are called for convenience 'Saturday ministries', Christians active in the worlds of entertainment, sport, the media, leisure and tourism.

This week we were offered a wonderful example of what it could be to live as a Christian young person. At the funeral of Anthony Walker, the black 18 year old tragically murdered, held in Liverpool Cathedral, he was described as showing 'Christian maturity far beyond his years'. His friend William Eborall, told with breaking voice how at primary school Anthony 'talked to me when nobody else would' and he did so because he was a Christian brought up by Christian parents. I couldn't help thinking that it is as important to teach our children to behave Christianly at school, as it is to teach them to say their prayers.

We must never become so preoccupied with the inner life of the church that we forget that our life as Christians is above all in the world with its different values and priorities and its profound secularity.

Let me finally say something about two facets of lay life – the spirituality and the Christian beliefs with which we need to be equipped in order to be Christians in the world.

Lay spirituality

The spiritual disciplines and expectations of the church can sometimes disable rather than empower us to understand and influence the structures of the world in which we live. We are for example encouraged to attend a Eucharist on saints' days, to make a retreat or to join the clergy in saying the daily offices. Now all of these are good things to do but they are essentially clerical disciplines. Only a fraction of the congregation can and does join in. We should be devising lay spiritual disciplines, which are more relevant to the pattern of our daily lives.

I was once invited to preach in Chichester Cathedral. It was in a Lent series on 'Prayer and the busy man' (those were unenlightened days before the introduction of inclusive language and we assumed that there was no such thing as 'a busy woman'!). I declined. My devotional life I decided was too haphazard to parade in the cathedral pulpit. My prayers took place mostly in the car on the Chichester bypass or while I was waiting for a difficult interview with a pupil, or parent – what we call arrow prayers. My Bible reading was largely confined to sermon preparation. Not since university days had I spent a regular daily quiet half hour each day in prayer and Bible reading. I felt I had nothing to say to the cathedral congregation. But of course I ought to have said precisely that because I suspect it reflected the experience of many busy people. How do we pray in the context of our lives, sandwiched between work, family, leisure activities, sleep and the television? And how does the church help us? And what about lay belief?

Lay belief

I sometimes hear people say: 'I don't suppose a Christian ought to think like that'. They mean that what they actually believe deep down does not conform to the creeds of the church, to what they believe the Bible says or what the rector expects them to believe. But belief is not what we ought to believe but what we do believe and if there is a gulf between the two then the church should be helping us to reconcile the two. I have a book called *Why Adult Christians don't learn*. Adult Christians don't learn, says the author, because they have learnt the creed or the catechism in their youth and have stopped learning at that point. But the belief of the laity is not static, fixed and sure.

Because we live in a challenging secular world our beliefs are constantly called into question. We are meeting people to whom many items in the Christian creeds are strange to the point of incomprehension. We cannot retreat to the ghetto of traditional statements. If our beliefs are not changing, adapting and growing then they are probably dying. Martin Luther was described as ' The sort of man who never knew what he believed until he heard himself saying it and never knew how much he believed until he heard himself being contradicted'. It is by articulating what we believe in the cut and thrust of debate with the people we meet at work or at the golf club that we hone and test our convictions. Lay belief is not a series of statements recited in church nor a catechism of answers learnt in childhood to questions people are no longer asking, but what we believe in our hearts and put to the test in the crucible of experience.

So we are not amateur, part-time, unpaid, non-clerical Christians. We are part of the *laos* of God called to live and serve Him in the strange, demanding world which he created and into which he calls us.

⚬

Forgiveness

Jesus... said to the paralysed man 'My son your sins are forgiven'. Mark 2.5

Authority to forgive sins

The incident described in this morning's gospel is a particularly vivid one. News has gone round that Jesus is back; staying it may be in Peter's house in Capernaum. A crowd including some Pharisees and lawyers has gathered, curious to hear Jesus, so many they have blocked the doorway and over-flowed into the street. The crowd gradually becomes aware that at the edge of the crowd there is a disturbance. Four men come into view carrying a paralysed man on a cheap mattress. They push their way through the crowd shouting, 'Make way, Mind your backs, Let's get through'. But eventually they give up, there's only one way they can reach Jesus. The next thing the crowd sees is the procession on the outside staircase leading to the roof. They watch in amazement as the men remove the twigs, matting, and earth which cover the beams, no doubt dropping debris below as they do so. They would incidentally not have done lasting damage to the roof – the covering would easily have been replaced.

By now nobody is listening to Jesus, perhaps he stopped speaking and watched too, as his friends lower the paralysed man until he lies at the feet of Jesus. There is a tense silence and then Jesus says: 'My son, your sins are forgiven you. Stand up, take up your bed and go home'. He gets up, picks up his bed and walks through the crowd. The crowd begins to murmur: 'What right has he to forgive sins? We've never seen anything like this before.'

What Jesus did was to offer to the paralysed man God's forgiveness entirely without conditions unlike the forgiveness which Jewish law offered. There were no terms attached, no ritual cleansing required, no sacrifice needed. The man was both forgiven and healed. But of course this was not a one off. Forgiveness of sins is at the heart of the Christian faith. This morning I want to try to answer the question, What is forgiveness?

First what forgiveness is not.

What forgiveness is not

Forgiveness is not God condoning sin, saying it doesn't matter like an over indulgent parent forgiving a spoilt child. Forgiveness is not making light of the evil in human beings and in the world. However you think of sin, it matters. Sin has been defined as self-centredness, as falling short of the mark. The psychologist Carl Jung described sin as the God Almightiness of humanity, putting ourselves in the position which only God should occupy. Sin destroys relationships and breaks up families. Lust, greed, pride and sloth spoil lives and destroy people. Sin matters. If forgiveness were condoning sin it would make nonsense of the character of God, who is holy love, acting in judgement and mercy. He is the benchmark against which we measure our own shortcomings and inadequacies.

Forgiveness is not getting rid of the consequences of sin. A child is born blind through the sexual sins of its parents. A teenager is maimed for life by a drunken driver. Through my youth I watched an uncle struggle for breath because he had been in a gas attack in the First World War. The parents of the blind child, the drunken driver and the German commander may ask forgiveness for their sin but the temporal consequences of their act are there for ever. 'Forgiveness', said Bernard Shaw, 'is a beggar's refuge. We must pay our debts'. 'There is no such thing as forgiveness', said T.H.Huxley, the man who invented the term agnostic.

Well if forgiveness isn't God condoning sin and if it doesn't rid us of the physical consequences of sin, what is it?

Restoring a broken relationship

Quite simply it is the restoring of a broken relationship. A quarrel causes strain, embarrassment, and above all estrangement between people. Forgiveness is not saying 'I'll pretend I never heard what you said', or 'It didn't matter what you did'. It involves saying 'What you did or said shall not stand between us'. The cost of forgiveness depends on the closeness of the relationship. You suspect the person who delivers your milk has been overcharging you; you can either say I'll give you another chance or alternatively you can change your supplier. The relationship is not a close one. But suppose a colleague ruins your business or breaks up your home, can you ever forgive? That is what a Christian says about God. We have ruined his business, broken up his world, killed his son yet he still says 'This shall not stand between us'. As Paul says in his second letter to the Corinthians ' …in Christ God was reconciling the world to himself'. (5.19)

The parable of the Prodigal Son is a timeless story of forgiveness. The Father did not forget the son's sin. He couldn't; the money, which formed his inheritance, had gone. He did not ignore the consequences of the prodigal's sin; he had returned weakened in body and tarnished in mind. Forgiveness meant taking the initiative in restoring the relationship, offering a new life – the best garment and the fatted calf. It involved the son's penitence and willingness to be forgiven; 'I am not worthy to be called your son' – which of us is? (Luke 15.11–32)

The forgiveness we are offered is similar: it is not cancelling a debt, not a word of grudging pardon but simply reception through faith back into the family.

What forgiveness does for us

Forgiveness makes us sensitive to sin. Every time we come to church there is an act of confession, an opportunity to recall, usually at the beginning of the service, what lies on our conscience, the things which ought to lie on our conscience but don't, the sins which we share with all people and need to confess corporately, the sins which are so deeply ingrained that we are scarcely aware of them. It is part of the service which we must never allow to become a tired formality.

The act of confession and hearing God's forgiveness declared make us more aware of our sins. We dare not be quite as censorious, insensitive, arrogant or resentful at others' success. Forgiveness must surely be a means of growing in grace as well as aware of how far we have to travel.

Forgiveness helps us to forgive other people. 'Forgive us our sins as we forgive those who sin against us', we pray in the Lord's Prayer. The startling truth is that we can only expect to be forgiven because we have already learnt what it is to forgive other people. But it is also true the other way round; once we have experienced forgiveness we have no alternative but to forgive other people. Forgiving our neighbour is both a condition and a consequence of our forgiveness by God.

Yet it is a hard lesson to learn. How often have we heard people say:

- I forgive him but I can't forget.
- I forgive but I shall never feel the same towards her again.
- I forgive but I hope he'll keep out of my way in future.
- I forgive but it's the last time.

Just put those utterances into the mouth of Jesus and you will see that they are not forgiveness at all. Forgiveness is the restoring of a broken relationship – the declaration this shall not stand between us; and it has no conditions attached.

Forgiveness heals. The story in this morning's gospel connects forgiveness with wholeness of body. In the ancient and medieval world many people believed that illness was the result of sin. If the man in the story believed that his paralysis was the result of sin then forgiveness may have been the condition of his physical recovery. We no longer make such a direct connection. But some illnesses may be the result of hidden tensions, concealed resentment, and repressed guilt. There is a mysterious connection between body and mind, diseases which we call psychosomatic. God can both forgive and heal. There is a verse in a hymn which reads: How can your pardon reach and bless/ the unforgiving heart?/ that broods on wrongs and will not let old bitterness depart?

One modern commentator suggests that Mark may have told the story of the forgiveness and healing of the paralysed man in the way he did because the situation was so similar to that in which they heard the story read. They were meeting in somebody's house to hear the word preached just as those people met to hear Jesus many years before. As they listened they too were open to receive the forgiveness and healing experienced by the paralysed man. As we meet not in a house but in church we don't expect anybody to enter through the roof but we should expect to receive the same forgiveness which the paralysed man experienced.

Ethics: why should I?

Romans 13.10 1 John 4.10

Last autumn some of us attended a course of Deanery lectures on the Christian approach to moral issues. The topics included war and peace, world poverty, marriage and divorce, homosexuality, euthanasia and genetic engineering. After the last lecture somebody commented to me that not one of the speakers had tried to establish a strong connection between Christian belief and moral consequences, between belief and behaviour, theology and practice. That is not really surprising since Christians have always found it difficult to agree about what constitutes Christian behaviour. This morning I want to consider some aspects of this important question..

A question

Let me start with a question which is on our lips or in our minds most days – why should I? Or it might be put negatively:why shouldn't I? It starts when we are very young. Why should I go to bed? I'm not tired yet. Why should I do my homework? Mr Smith never checks and Amanda gets away with it every week. Why shouldn't I smoke? All the boys in my class do. But the question doesn't stop when we grow up though we may ask it silently rather than out aloud. Why should I pay my television licence if I can get away with it? Why shouldn't I use my influence to get the job I want or the contract which will benefit my firm? Why should I? Or to put it in a more sophisticated form, as a Christian what principles should guide my conduct?

Three answers

There are three answers which cover the bulk of the choices we have to make and they are answers which we share with those who have no Christian commitment.

First of all there's *compulsion.* If I own a car, or a motorbike I must tax and insure it, drive it on the left hand side of the road, observe the speed limit and carry L plates until I've passed the test. Why? – compulsion: the law says so and I shall be prosecuted if I don't. If I join the golf club or the youth club I must pay my subscription and obey the rules. Why? – compulsion: because those are the conditions of joining.

Then there's *custom*. Why watch *Coronation Street, Neighbours, Newsnight, University Challenge* or *Match of the Day*. Custom: my friends do and I need something to talk about at school or in the office. Why wear jeans and a tee shirt or suit and tie? Custom: everybody else is and I shall be out of place if I don't.

Finally, *choice*. Where did you go for your holiday this year? Was it the Costa del Sol, Euro-Disney, Tenerife, walking in Snowdonia, or your usual visit to Ilfracombe? Why should I? Choice: I like it like that. How did you spend yesterday: playing or watching football, cutting the lawn, shopping in Southampton? Why? – choice: I just like it like that.

Now the great majority of our decisions fall into one or more of those categories. Our choices, including many moral choices are the result of compulsion, custom or choice. There are however some for which the three Cs are insufficient.

Another dimension

We decide to make a substantial contribution to cancer relief or to an appeal for children suffering from famine in Africa. We opt for what we know to be right conduct in the face of overwhelming temptation. We apply for a job, which involves real sacrifice, a reduction of our present standard of living, a lower salary, reduced esteem and less comfort. We deliberately make friends with somebody who is isolated and unclubbable. It is here that the categories of compulsion, custom and choice break down. There is no *compulsion* to do any of these things. It is certainly not the *custom* of those around us to act in this way. And unaided *choice* would scarcely lead us to such an act of self-sacrifice.

We think I suppose of people like Mother Theresa of Calcutta. What was it which led her to serve for a lifetime the destitute, the dirty and the diseased in Calcutta, one of the most appalling cities in the world? Let me give you a less spectacular example. A girl I knew at Cambridge became a doctor and has spent her life in hospitals in Africa, for over twenty years in Sierra Leone, where her Christmas letters year after year have made heart-rending reading. But there she stayed until she retired a year or two ago and even now she is to be found supporting good causes; marching, collecting, lobbying. She has lived a life of profound self-sacrifice. Why did she do it? Certainly not compulsion, nor custom, nor ordinary human choice. There is another dimension altogether here.

What the Bible says about behaviour

As Christians we turn to the Bible and ask what it has to say to us about the moral choices we make. The Old Testament answer to Why should I? Is quite simple. It gives us rules to obey. The Ten Commandments are only the tip of an iceberg. By the time of Jesus almost every possible situation was covered by a law. Jesus as we know found himself at odds with the Pharisees because he was impatient of their legalistic interpretation of Jewish laws. Last Sunday's gospel contained the story of Jesus healing on the Sabbath contrary to Jewish law.

The New Testament is at first sight disappointingly thin as a guide to conduct. The Beatitudes are not new laws for Christians to observe. What Jesus is reported as saying is not: 'You must be merciful, you must be pure in heart, you must show mercy', but something rather different – you will be happy if … you are merciful, pure in heart, peacemakers'. It's up to you to decide. St Paul offers lists of vices to avoid and virtues to cultivate but they are only examples, not an exhaustive list. He has no new version of the Ten Commandments to offer to the young churches.

It is surely odd that there is so little ethical content in the New Testement. In fact the clue to the New Testament's approach to the question, why should I?, is precisely in its inadequacy. The New Testament offers us not a new law, a code of conduct for Christians to adhere to but a person and a principle; the person of Christ and the principle of love. These are the answers to the question, why should I?

The person of Christ and the principle of love

You remember how Jesus was once asked by a lawyer who set out to trap him, which was the most important commandment. It was a bit like those questions about which quality you most value in a car – speed, safety, economy, reliability, appearance. Would Jesus say – don't steal, or don't commit adultery, or honour your parents. But Jesus goes behind all of them and replies *Love God, love your neighbour. There is no other commandment greater than these.* (Mark 12.28-31)

Well then, what is love? Do you remember those examination questions which say 'Define the following words and give an example of each'. The way to answer them is to tackle the second part of the question first. Think of an example and then work back to the definition. If you want to know what love is you look at Jesus, to love in action and that gives you your definition.

As a parent you may have been faced with the question from your son or daughter reading a book for homework, 'Mum/Dad, what's the meaning of …' Stalling for time you say, 'What's the context?' because with your greater experience, even if the word is unfamiliar, you will be able to deduce the meaning from how it's used. Well, love in the New Testament is like that. You recognise it when you see it in context, in the life and death of Jesus. It is not an abstract to be defined but something concrete to be seen in action.

When St Paul wrote the famous hymn to love in the first letter to the Corinthians chapter 13 it has been suggested that what he was doing was composing a pen portrait of Jesus, something derived from his life-long meditation on the person who had encountered him on the road to Damascus. How's this for a description of Jesus?

> Love is patient; love is kind, love is not envious, or boastful or arrogant or rude. It does not insist on its own way; it is not irritable or resentful; it does not rejoice in wrongdoing, but rejoices in the truth. It bears all things, believes all things, hopes all things, endures all things. Love never ends. (4–8)

Paul it has been said uses a sledgehammer to crack a nut. When he wants to urge the Corinthians to give generously to the collection he says; 'You know the grace of our Lord Jesus Christ, how for our sakes he became poor that by his poverty we might become rich'. (2 Corinthians 8.9) When he wants to tell the Philippians not to be conceited he says 'Have this mind in you which was also in Christ Jesus … he emptied himself taking the form of a slave...' (2.5,7) So when we are faced with the decisions of life we need the sledge-hammer of the love of Christ. Why should I forgive my neighbour? The love of Christ. Why should I give generously to a cancer appeal or for those desperate children in Africa? The love of Christ. Why should I befriend the unclubbable and the isolated? The love of Christ.

Let me return for a moment to those deanery lectures. Some people may have expected that solutions to complex ethical questions could be drawn out from the Bible and basic Christian beliefs. But the same principle is at work; the New Testament does not contain rules on divorce, peace and war, poverty, genetic engineering, homosexuality or anything else though many people believe it does. It offers on these subjects too the principle of love and the person of Christ and bids us set to work to tease out what these mean for our world and our culture.

I started with a question Why should I? I suggested that most situations can be answered with three C's – *compulsion, custom and choice* but for the harder decisions, for the direction of our choices, for the crucial situations we need something more and for a Christian that is not a new law, a further set of commandments but a person and a principle.

Let me finish with a well-known saying of St Augustine and two New Testament texts. From St Augustine: *Love God and do what you like –* because loving God will lead you to do the right thing. From the letter to the Romans chapter13 verse10, *The whole law is summed up in love.* And if you want to know what love is the first letter of John chapter 4 verse 10 *The love I speak of is not our love for God but the love he showed us in sending his son as the remedy for the defilement of our sins.*

Infant Baptism

Baptism and confirmation

If I asked you which you remember more clearly, your baptism or your confirmation, you would probably reply, confirmation. Your baptism probably took place when you were a baby and it is only memorable in family folklore if you screamed throughout or the Vicar dropped you. You were probably confirmed on the other hand when you were an impressionable teenager and you may remember the bishop, the church and perhaps how you felt at the time.

If I asked you a second question, which was the more important event in your Christian life -your baptism or your confirmation? – you would probably give the same answer. At your baptism promises, of which you were wholly unaware, were made on your behalf, by your parents and godparents. Before your confirmation on the other hand, you went to classes, made your own vows, decided you wanted to follow Christ and become a full member of his church, and afterwards you began to receive Holy Communion.

But you would be wrong. In the New Testament, in the history of the church and in its theology it is baptism which is central. In fact the New Testament has no reference to confirmation at all; it was not practised in the church until the fourth century; it is not to this day practised in the Orthodox churches of the east, and theologians cannot agree on its precise meaning. It is baptism which is one of the two gospel sacraments, one of the two things which Jesus commanded his followers to do. Baptism is the sacrament of beginning in the Christian life; Holy Communion, the sacrament of continuing fellowship. We read as the gospel this morning the last words which, according to Matthew's gospel, Jesus spoke after the Resurrection: ' Go and make disciples of all nations, baptizing them in the name of the Father and the Son and the Holy Spirit' (28.29).

Baptism in the Acts of the Apostles

If you want to see how central to the gospel baptism was in the early church you only have to look at the Acts of the Apostles where there are 27 references to baptism. It was the invariable accompaniment to the preaching of the gospel, the natural consequence of hearing and believing, and the gateway to membership of the church.

Here for example is the response of those who heard Peter's first sermon: 'Those who welcomed the message were baptised and that day about 3000 people were added to the church'. (Acts 2.41) In the Acts of the Apostles chapter eight Philip preaches the gospel to the Ethiopian court official on the road from Jerusalem to Gaza. He receives the good news and he says to Philip: 'Look here is water, what is to prevent my being baptised?' He stops the chariot and Philip baptizes him. (Acts 8.36-38) We are all familiar with the story of the call of Paul on the Damascus road but less so with the sequel. Paul's call is not complete with that dramatic religious experience, but only when he has been welcomed into the Christian community by Ananias and baptised. (Acts 9.18)

Why infant baptism?

'Wait a minute', you will say: 'If baptism follows the preaching of the gospel and is the response to faith and commitment, why is it that the church baptises children who are too young to hear or respond to the gospel? Surely those 3000 people listening to Peter, the Ethiopian court official and St Paul were all adults who had heard, responded and decided to follow Christ?' And of course there *are* some Christians who refuse to baptise children. The Baptist church in particular practises adult baptism. People are baptised in response to a profession of faith and by immersion, which the Baptist church believes is the biblical command. Why then do the great majority of Christians – Catholic, Orthodox, Anglican and Reformed alike, practise infant baptism?

There are three strands to the answer – biblical, theological and pastoral.

Biblical
The church described in Acts may have baptised children; we cannot be sure. There are two places in the Acts of the Apostles chapter 16 where a

whole family is baptised, and it seems likely that this would have included children. At Philippi Paul preached to some women by the river outside the town. One of them was Lydia, a dealer in purple cloth. And Luke says 'The Lord opened her heart to listen eagerly to what was said by Paul. ...She and her whole household were baptised'. Later Paul and Silas escape from gaol as the result of an earthquake and the gaoler is so impressed that he too becomes a Christian and Luke says 'He and his whole household were baptised without delay' (vv.15 & 33). Surely that too would have included his children?

Many people believe that the story told in the gospels of Jesus receiving the children implies that children should be welcomed as full members of the church and the story was perhaps used at baptisms. 'Let the little children come to me and do not stop them, for it is to such that the Kingdom of God belongs' (Matthew 19.14,15).

Theological

The second reason why we baptise children is theological. The central truth of the gospel, to which infant baptism bears witness, is that Christ chooses us rather than our choosing him. The gospel is offer before it is demand. I was baptised as a baby not because I had decided to believe but because God loved me before ever I could respond. The important thing about baptism is not what we do but what he does: it is the sacrament of grace. And that profound theological truth could not be better demonstrated than by the baptism of a helpless infant. The service of baptism used in the Methodist church spells this out. The minister says to those to be baptised: 'For you Jesus came into the world; for you he lived and showed God's love....all this for you, before you could know anything about it. In your Baptism the word of scripture is fulfilled: 'We love because he first loved us'.[1] 'Christ's death' says Alan Richardson ' was the baptism of the whole human race. Christ is the saviour not only of the church but of the world'.

Pastoral

The third reason why we baptise infants is pastoral and brings our theology down to earth. The church has baptised infants from the earliest years because it could not do otherwise. Membership of the body of Christ is too good to be restricted to adults. Our response to the grace of God must be to share it with all and in particular with the new members as they join our family. So just as we share with our children all the good things in life so we share with them full membership of the Body of Christ through baptism.

We don't wait until they grow up to feed our children. We start at once. We don't wait until they can understand before we talk to them; that is how they learn to speak. We don't wait until they are fully coordinated before we buy them a football and the appropriate strip.

So baptism is the beginning of the journey, the sign that children are the recipients of all the love and care which the Christian community can offer them. In the words of the Liturgical Commission, baptism as not a *moment* but a *process*, not something which happens once and is forgotten but something which is the beginning of the Christian way.

So this morning Heather and Dermot have brought Peter Francis for baptism. We rejoice with them and we share together in this sacrament of the grace of God who loves us before ever we love him. We shall welcome Peter Francis into the Lord's family. And as we do so we shall once more renew the baptismal vows made on our behalf when we too were babes in arms.

1. *The Methodist Worship Book* Methodist Publishing House 1999 pp.92-93. I am grateful to my brother for drawing my attention to this reference.

BIBLICAL TOPICS

Is the Bible the Word of God?

You search the scriptures because you think that in them you have eternal life; and it is they which testify on my behalf. You refuse to come to me to have life. John 5.39-40
The word became flesh and lived among us. John 1.14a

In 1861 Dr J.W. Burgon, an Oxford theologian preached a sermon in the church of St Mary the Virgin, the university church in Oxford which contained these words:

> The Bible is none other than the voice of him that sitteth upon the throne. Every book of it, every chapter of it, every verse of it, every word of it, every syllable of it (where are we to stop?), every letter of it, is the direct utterance of the most high. The Bible is none other than the Word of God, not some part of it more, some part of it less, but all alike the utterance of him who sitteth upon the throne, faultless, unerring, supreme.[1]

This is an extreme statement of the view held by many Christians in the middle of the nineteenth century. The Bible was God's word, infallible, verbally inspired, all parts of equal authority and containing guidance on all important matters of belief and behaviour. It is a view held today by very few Christians. Why I wonder is this view of the Bible no longer held?

Reasons for abandoning the literalist view of the Bible

The repercussions of Darwin's Origin of Species
In 1859 two years before Dr Burgon preached his sermon Charles Darwin published his famous book *The Origin of Species*. It set out in great detail with corroborative evidence the theory of the evolution of animal species including humankind through natural selection. It was incompatible with the literal truth of the creation of the world and the origin of human life set out in the early chapters of the book of Genesis. Archbishop James Ussher, in his *Sacred Chronology* published in 1660, had calculated the date of the creation as 4004 BC and the date still appeared in many copies of the Bible. According to Darwin the world was millions of years old. The literal Adam and Eve created out of Adam's rib, the Garden of Eden and the Flood were all now seen as myths of a primitive people.

It was the beginning of questioning of Bible stories by ordinary people. 'O God', prayed one old lady allegedly, 'Grant that evolution be not true and if it is give us the grace to hush it up'. By 1870 the scientific view had won and its opponents were on the defensive. Well over 100 years later that rearguard action is still being fought mostly but not exclusively in the United States where there are schools where science lessons may not include the teaching of evolution.

The impact of Biblical criticism

In the second half of the nineteenth century the Bible was submitted to the same close critical scrutiny as other ancient texts. Just as the challenge of science was exemplified by *The Origin of Species* so the issue of biblical criticism was pinpointed by *Essays and Reviews* published only a few months after Darwin's book. The difference was that all but one of its contributors were influential Anglican clergymen. It caused an even bigger crisis for the Church of England than had *The Origin of Species.*

Scholars now maintained that the first five books of the Bible were not written by Moses. There are two accounts of Creation and the five books of the Pentateuch, as scholars call them, consist of a number of documents put together much later. Isaiah consists of three books written at different times. The Old Testament prophets didn't foresee Jesus but instead Jesus used the Old Testament to understand and describe his own ministry.

The gospels too were studied carefully. They were no longer seen as biographies of Jesus, which had been written independently but instead Luke and Matthew had used Mark and had made changes to some of incidents to fit their theological purpose.

It became hard to believe that the Bible was a book God had dictated in the way Dr Burgon believed. It had been composed by human beings working under God's inspiration maybe but not at his dictation. It appeared to have passed through the same processes of compilation and corruption as other ancient texts.

A changing morality

Until the end of the eighteenth century the morality of the Bible was largely unquestioned. By the nineteenth century many people began to have doubts. Could it be that the God and Father of our Lord Jesus Christ would rain brimstone on Sodom and Gomorrah. (Genesis 19.24-26). Was he likely to condone the murder of Sisera with a workman's mallet and a tent peg, (Judges 5.26) or the mauling of 42 small boys by two she bears for calling Elisha by his nickname, Baldhead? (2 Kings 2.23-25) Was it the Christian God who had allowed Samuel 'to hew Agag in pieces before the Lord'? (1 Samuel 15.33)

As people reflected from within the Christian faith on such cruel and barbarous events it seemed clear that the God of the Old Testament fell below the moral standards of the nineteenth century let alone the perfect love of God as exemplified in Jesus Christ. George Macdonald wrote a poem which included these lines:

> Here lie I, Martin Elginbrod,
> Have mercy on my soul, O God,
> As I would do if I were God,
> And you were Martin Elginbrod.[2]

The impact of Darwinian science, historical criticism of the Bible and moral reflection all made it impossible for thoughtful people any longer to regard the Bible as literally the Word of God.

The Word of God incarnate

How then should we regard the Bible? The problem is that the church has never replaced the literalist view with an accepted alternative. It is because we do not have an alternative key to the scriptures that many of us feel guilty in rejecting literalism.

In the words from John's gospel which I have taken as a text Jesus is quoted as attacking an exaggerated faith in the Old Testament. 'You search the scriptures', he says ' because you think that in them you have eternal life... You refuse to come to me to have life'. Jesus is saying that it is in him, not in the words of Old Testament scripture, that life will be found. The key to the Bible is Jesus Christ. The Word of God is not a book, not a spoken word or a written word but a lived word. God speaks to us supremely in the person of Jesus Christ. The Bible is his word in so far as it witnesses to him.

The Bible was written in and for a Middle Eastern culture whose values could scarcely have been more different from our own. We have to undertake the difficult process of translating what the Bible had to say to a remote culture into the currency of the twenty first century. If we fail to do so we shall end up with a faith which is simply an anachronism.

Yet we so often fall back on the words of the Bible. Here are two examples where in recent years people have justified practices from the Bible which most people would regard as sub-Christian. The subordination of women, and until the 1990s their exclusion from the priesthood of the Church of England, was justified by appeal to the words in the First Letter to Timothy, 'I permit no woman to teach or to have authority over a man... For Adam was formed first then Eve' (2.11–15). Were those words written for

British churches in the twenty first century or for a Mediterranean culture in the first century?

In 1986 the Court of Human Rights outlawed corporal punishment in schools. A group of Christian teachers have since tried to gain exemption from the ruling because they consider that the Bible commands them to use corporal punishment to discipline children. ' Those who spare the rod, hate their children, but those who love them are diligent to discipline them' says the writer of Proverbs (13.24)

There are plenty of other examples from earlier periods of history. Slavery was justified for centuries because it was an acceptable institution in the Roman world in the first century and therefore assumed in many parts of the Bible. The Dutch Reformed Church for many years quoted the Old Testament as defending the subjugation of black people because the book of Joshua described them as 'hewers of wood and drawers of water'. (9. 21, 27). In the Middle Ages Christians were forbidden to lend money at interest because it was forbidden in the Old Testament (Exodus 22.25, Deuteronomy 23.19-20, Leviticus 25. 35, 38.) Jews were permitted to do so and became the moneylenders of Europe.

No the Bible is not the Word of God – God did not and does not communicate with us directly through the pages of a book but in a person, the person of Jesus Christ

I have a book on my shelves called *Why Jesus never wrote a book*. If this sermon had a title it would be *Why God never wrote a book*. The answer is that he chose to disclose himself in a person and he goes on disclosing himself in that same Jesus to whom scripture bears witness.

1. Quoted in A.M.G. Stevenson *The rise and decline of English Modernism* SPCK 1984 p.321
2. Quoted in H.G.Wood *Belief and unbelief since 1850* CUP 1954 p.33

Wrestling Jacob

Genesis 32.13-31

Jacob

It is hard for us to identify with many of the characters of the Old Testament. They are supermen – only occasionally superwomen – cast in a mould which sets them well beyond our reach. They are leaders like

Abraham, Moses or Joshua, kings like Saul, David or Solomon, men of prophetic insight and spiritual sensitivity like Isaiah, Jeremiah or Amos. Jacob is the exception; he is more accessible, built on more ordinary lines. He is a man of the world, exemplifying all too clearly shortcomings which we recognise – envious, selfish, a man on the make, with a flair for an unscrupulous bargain. He is like the people we read about in the business pages of the quality dailies or meet perhaps in professional life, a Rupert Murdoch, or Conrad Black.

Let me recall the story which lies behind the Old Testament reading. Jacob was born the younger of twins. His father was Isaac, his mother Rebecca and his twin brother Esau. From the beginning he was his mother's favourite. As a boy he cheated Esau out of his rights as elder brother by offering him a meal when Esau came back ravenous from hunting. As a youth, helped by Rebecca, Jacob again cheats Esau out of his dying father's blessing by impersonating the hairy arms of his brother.

That was the beginning of a rift in the family. Esau threatened Jacob's life and so he fled and went to live with his uncle Laban. During the next 20 years he married first Leah, Laban's elder daughter and then Rachel the younger daughter whom he had loved all along (29.15-30) He prospered and his flocks multiplied as a result of a bit of crafty selective breeding described by the writer of Genesis (30.31–43) Now in middle life he is going home but with considerable trepidation. Will Esau let bygones be bygones or will he still nurse a grudge after all these years? Will he again threaten Jacob's life? Jacob takes no chances. He divides his flocks into two hoping to hold on to at least one half. He sends lavish presents and ingratiating messages. He asks the help of God in prayers which are designed to flatter and cajole the Almighty.

That's the background to the Old Testament passage. It could be the plot of a novel about the Australian outback or the American west. It could be the story line of a TV blockbuster. It comes from a book of the Old Testament where legend, saga, history and poetry blend in the dramatic stories of the patriarchs.

Encounter in the river Jabbok

Now Jacob takes his wives and children, his herds and flocks across the river Jabbok. And says the writer ' *Jacob was left alone and a man wrestled with him until day break*'. (v.24). It is one of the great stories of the Old Testament which we can interpret on a number of levels. At one level it is mythology: Jacob wrestles with the demon who was supposed to live in every river. We can interpret it psychologically: Jacob struggles with his own inner life at this moment of mid-life crisis. Or we can see the story as part of Jacob's religious experience as he wrestles with God: '*He called the place Peniel, for I have seen God face to face*'. (v.30)

How do we encounter God?

Let me suggest three aspects of Jacob's encounter with God which speak to us.

The source of Jacob's encounter

If I asked you how you expect to meet God you would probably reply through prayer, through reading the Bible, through the fellowship of a house group, through the weekly Eucharist. And of course you would be right: God does reach us through what the General Thanksgiving calls 'the means of grace'. But these are not the only ways God reaches us. Some of us even find that church services leave us cold and there are times when prayer seems like talking to ourselves.

God also reaches us as he did Jacob. He met Jacob in his moment of crisis as he has to come to terms with himself. He must recognise the twister he has always been, the sharp practice of which he has often been guilty. God speaks to him through the stormy relations with his brother, through the prosperity which has come his way but which is now in jeopardy, through this mid-life family crisis.

Perhaps God speaks to us in similar ways. We hear him speaking to us as we recognise our limitations and our abilities, the pride and selfishness we have never been able to conquer, as well as the generosity, the love and compassion of which we are capable. He speaks to us in the disappointments which come our way or perhaps through the chronic illness of a relation which we must learn to live with. He speaks to us through relationships with family and friends, through the plans we make for the future. It is now many years since we learnt from Paul Tillich perhaps via Bishop John Robinson to talk about God as 'the ground of Being', as 'ultimate concern'. The source of our encounter with God may be in part through the ordinary experiences of living our daily lives.

The nature of Jacob's encounter

It is a weird and eerie story based on primitive folklore. A man crosses the Jabbok at dead of night, the river demon seizes him, and they struggle in the murky waters until Jacob cries out 'Tell me your name'. The demon refuses to divulge his identity and Jacob holds on. It is a story which is not just Jacob's but that of Everyman and Everywoman.

We have sometimes been taught that the authentic note of religious faith is submission and obedience to what the Bible or the church teaches about belief and behaviour We must we are told no longer rely on our own strength. Billy Graham popularised the hymn *'Blessed assurance Jesus is mine'*. The second and third verses both begin *Perfect submission*... For some people perhaps faith does mean assurance and submission. But for many the image of Jacob wrestling in the river Jabbok is closer to our experience.

The profoundest religious literature of the twentieth century had about it a note of passionate enquiry, striving to make sense of a world, which seems to be heading for disaster, which we are powerless to halt. I think of Dietrich Bonhoeffer's *Letters and Papers from Prison* or Harry Williams' autobiography *Some Day I'll Find You*.

There are so many issues where we have to wrestle and where there are no easy answers. Should Christians support the recent war in Iraq? Is divorce always wrong? How should a Christian who is gay behave and how should the church regard him? We need to wrestle in the river, seeking to discern what God has to say to us. God is in the questions not just there to provide the answers. It is of the very nature of religious faith to wrestle with God.

One word of warning. Because faith involves wrestling in the river there is no excuse for remaining on the bank. Jacob hung on through the night. Bonhoeffer died a martyr in Nazi Germany just before the war ended. Harry Williams went through a traumatic nervous breakdown before he was able to resume his ministry and preach again.

The result of Jacob's encounter

May I urge you to read again the whole of the Jacob story from Genesis chapter 25 to chapter 33? After the encounter at Peniel described in chapter 32 there is a dramatic change. The shifty smart Alec of his youth and middle years is changed. Jacob is first of all reconciled with Esau and they are described outdoing each other in consideration for one another. Jacob is given a new name. We all know I am sure that in many ancient civilisations a name is of profound significance. Jacob is a name meaning 'supplanter'. As a result of his encounter in the Jabbok he becomes Israel, God's warrior, the perseverer with God.

The test of our encounter with God is the sort of people we become. Like Jacob we are called to be reconcilers, like Jacob we become useful, we gain a sense of purpose. Ordinary selfish people demonstrate greater love, care and understanding. I recall a sentence I once read in *The New Statesman*: 'He was one of those people naïve enough to believe that religion makes a difference to the way a person behaves' – what an indictment yet we all recognise the truth of the claim in ourselves as well as in others.

'Wrestling Jacob'

Jacob's request for the demon's name was not answered, though we assume that it was God with whom he wrestled. It was left to Charles Wesley to answer the question and to Christianise the Old Testament story in one of his finest hymns. When it was first published in 1742 it was entitled *'Wrestling Jacob'*. It begins:

> Come O thou traveller unknown,
> Whom still I hold but cannot see;
> My company before is gone,
> And I am left alone with thee;
> With thee all night I mean to stay
> And wrestle till the break of day.

It goes on:

> But who I ask thee, who art thou?
> Tell me thy name and tell me now.

And the final verse reads:

> In vain thou strugglest to get free
> 'Tis Love! 'tis Love! Thou diedst for me!
> I hear thy whisper in my heart!
> The morning breaks, the shadows flee;
> Pure universal Love thou art:
> To me, to all, thy mercies move;
> The nature and thy name is Love.

The mystery of the universe with which Jacob wrestled is Love.
Religious belief is not easy – perhaps it never was, nor was it intended to be.

> For its source we look within as God addresses us as we are.
> For its nature it requires in our generation wrestling and striving.
> And its result is to become different sort of people.

The Lord is my shepherd

Psalm 23, Ezekiel 34. 7-16, John 10.7-16, 1Peter 5.1–4

The world of the Bible now lies between 2000 and 3000 years in the past. It is moreover a Middle Eastern world and one which was chiefly pastoral and agricultural, all features which differentiate it from the predominantly industrial society of twenty first century western Europe in which we live. Not surprisingly therefore the metaphors and similes which the Bible employs are difficult to relate to our world. And yet there is no image more loved by Christians than that of the shepherd and the sheep. It is a profoundly Biblical image. There are over 200 references to sheep and over 100 to shepherds in the Bible, many of them in the Old Testament.

It is an image that has inspired some of our best-loved hymns. There are at least four hymns derived from Psalm 23. *The Lord's my shepherd, I'll not want,* is a Scottish metrical psalm usually sung to the equally loved tune Crimond; *The God of love my shepherd is* comes from George Herbert's collection *The Temple* published in 1633 and in the nineteenth century Herbert Williams Baker wrote *The king of love my shepherd is.* The fourth shepherd hymn much less well known except by Methodists is Charles Wesley's *Thou shepherd of Israel and mine, the joy and desire of my heart,* a mystical hymn of great depth.

Contemporary images of sheep and shepherds

But though much loved the picture of the shepherd and his sheep is not an easy one for us. What I wonder do people brought up in Hackney or Handsworth make of the Lord as a shepherd? We tried a few years ago to update some of these pastoral images by supplementing them with images from the contemporary world. Richard Jones, a Methodist minister wrote a hymn which was popular for a time but seems to have dropped out of use: 'God of concrete, God of steel, / God of piston and of wheel, / God of pylon, God of steam. / God of girder and of beam. / God of atom, God of mine, / all the world of power is thine'. But a God of concrete and steel, is too reminiscent of the tower blocks of the 1960s and does not have the Biblical resonance of *The Lord is my shepherd.*

But even if we come from the country the image of shepherds and sheep does not mean the same as it did to the biblical world. I am not at all sure for example that I want to be described as a sheep. The sheep I come across are usually fat, and woolly, always eating, rather stupid and prone to follow the one in front. And my picture of a shepherd is drawn from the television programme *One Man and his Dog* or on my observation of shepherds in the Lake District or the Yorkshire Dales. A shepherd today is somebody whose skill lies more in controlling his sheep dog than caring for his sheep, in ensuring that however reluctantly, they reach pen or pasture. There's not much there to convey to me a vivid image of Jesus as the Good Shepherd.

Sheep and shepherds in the Bible

If we are to recover the power and meaning of the Biblical picture of sheep and shepherds we need to recognise just how different was their role in the economy of the Bible lands two millennia and more ago. They were as central to the Biblical world as they were to England in the Middle Ages. We all know that the Lord Chancellor sits on the Woolsack in the House of Lords and that some of our most beautiful medieval churches in East Anglia and the Cotswolds are called 'wool' churches because they owed their size and splendour to the benefactions of rich wool merchants.

The sheep of the Bible were bred for wool rather than meat. They were nimble, intelligent and sensitive as well as smaller. I don't mind being described as a sheep in this biblical sense!

The place of the shepherd in the Bible was also different from his counterpart today. He had a key role. David was called from being a shepherd to be king of Israel. Amos was called from being a shepherd to become a prophet. 'I was no prophet, nor a prophet's son ...and the Lord took me from following the flock', he writes describing his call. (Amos 7.14-15). There were no sheep dogs. It was the shepherd who tended the flock and did it 24 hours a day. So when we use the image of sheep and shepherd we must picture the shepherds of Israel not the shepherds of Yorkshire or the Lake District.

The Biblical shepherd and the Good Shepherd

Let's reflect on four characteristics of the Biblical shepherd which serve to remind us that *the Lord is my shepherd.*

The shepherd stays close to his flock. The hills were unfenced, the pasture thin, the terrain rocky, the haunt of hyenas, lions and bears. The shepherd must stay close to his sheep day and night for their mere survival. Without his vigilance they would perish in hours. The Lord is my shepherd.

The shepherd leads his sheep. He did not drive them nor direct them from a distance. He didn't whistle nor control them through a sheep dog. He led from the front and they followed. He must be prepared for sleepless nights. He was often a worn, weather beaten figure. The Lord is my shepherd.

The shepherd knows his sheep They were not just anonymous faces. He recognised them by oddities of temperament, distinctive markings which he had noted when they were born, individual characteristics which they might inherit from earlier generations. He counted them at least twice a day. Jesus' parable of the lost sheep draws on the shepherd discovering that there were only ninety-nine when there should have been a hundred. He searched until he found the lost sheep, stuck perhaps on a precipitous rock face. He carried the lost sheep home on his shoulder. (Luke 15.6) The Lord is my shepherd.

The shepherd defends his sheep. Do you recall David the shepherd lad about to fight the giant of a man Goliath? Saul sees this slender youth and says 'You're just a boy and Goliath has been a warrior from his youth'; in effect 'You'll never do it'. David replies: 'Your servant used to keep sheep for his father and whenever a lion or a bear came, and took a lamb from the flock, I went after it and struck it down, rescuing the lamb from its mouth, and if it turned against me I would catch it by the jaw, strike it down and kill it'. (1 Samuel 17.33-35) Recall too Jesus' saying 'I am the door of the sheep'. The sheep passed under the shepherd's crook to safety in the sheepfold. 'I lay down my life for the sheep'. The Lord is my shepherd.

Here then is a picture of Jesus as the Good Shepherd who is with his flock, leads, knows and defends his sheep. That role is endorsed in the most sustained Old Testament passage about sheep, in Ezekiel chapter 34. In a sentence of great power and eloquence Ezekiel denounces the leaders of Israel as shepherds who have not cared for the flock. 'You have not strengthened the weak, you have not healed the sick, you have not bound up the injured, you have not brought back the straggler, you have not sought the lost. So they were scattered because there was no shepherd and scattered they became food for all the wild animals. (Ezekiel 34. 4-6)

In the New Testament Jesus does not denounce his followers but instead calls them to shepherd his flock. In that moving scene by the Sea of Galilee after the Resurrection described in John's gospel Jesus delivers the well known threefold call to Peter: 'Feed my lambs...Tend my sheep... Feed my sheep.' (John 21.15-17) The writer of the First Letter of Peter takes up the same command when he says: 'I exhort the elders among you to tend the flock of God that is in your charge....Do not lord it over those in your charge, but be examples to the flock. And when the chief shepherd comes you will gain the crown of glory which fades not away'. (1 Peter 5.2-4)

The Good Shepherd and Christian ministry

It is from such passages as these that the image of the shepherd has become central to Christian ministry. Some Christian denominations, particularly those which arose from the Reformation, describe their clergy as pastor – shepherd of God's flock. We speak of pastoral care as among the church's most important functions. In the Church of England the bishop carries a crozier, a symbol of his place as the chief shepherd of the sheep. The service for the ordination of priests includes these words: 'A priest is called by God ... as servant and shepherd among the people to whom he is sent.....He must set the Good Shepherd always before him as the pattern of his calling, caring for the people committed to his charge'... and later ' the treasure now to be entrusted to you is Christ's own flock'.

So despite the difficulty of translating the image of the shepherd and the sheep into twenty first century terms we continue to value the Biblical model it gives us of Christian ministry. It is a ministry entrusted not just to the ordained full time priesthood of the church but to all of us as we seek to share in the ministry which the Good Shepherd gives to his whole church.

Ecclesiastes

Vanity of vanities says the Teacher. Vanity of vanities! All is vanity. Ecclesiastes 1.2

The trouble with the New Testament is that it was written in the glow of an evangelical revival. Much of it rings with joy and certainty. The Old Testament is different. It is the story of a Long March through a thousand years of a nation's history. The skies are sometimes blue and the terrain smooth but often the going is rough and the people stumble 'amid encircling gloom'. The Old Testament is the experience of Everyman; a story of disobedience, suffering and perplexity. There is no more dramatic example than the book of Ecclesiastes.

You will find it tucked between Proverbs and Isaiah. It was described as the bedside book of the twentieth century and that can now be extended to the twenty first century. It is a tract for the post-modern world. It is one of the few books of the Bible which are not represented in the Sunday readings in the *Common Worship* lectionary. You have probably never heard a sermon on it and not surprisingly.

Author

Ecclesiastes was written by an elderly well-to-do Jew whose name we do not know, who adopts the device of writing as though he were Solomon, the son of David. (1.1) He lived near Jerusalem during the Greek occupation about 200 BC. The society of his day was corrupt and unjust. He was a pessimist and a sceptic. The best known verse is 'Vanity of vanities, all is vanity', translated in the New English Bible, 'Emptiness, emptiness all is emptiness'. (1.2) He uses the Hebrew word *hebel*, translated vanity or emptiness, no less than 38 times.

Contents

The twelve chapters of his carefully structured book contain accounts of his attempts to find meaning in life. He tries learning. He will become knowledgeable and cultured, the wisest man in the world. He will study and read until nothing is a closed book to him. But it is pointless, 'The more a man knows the more he has to suffer... of the making many books there is no end and much study is a weariness of the flesh...'(12.12) He turns to pleasure; he builds houses, lays out gardens, and collects curios and antiques. He sets out to become the richest man in Jerusalem and devotes himself to wine, women and song. But that too turns to ashes: 'I considered all that my hands had done and the toil I had spent in doing it and again all was vanity and a chasing of the wind.' (2.11).

So he realises that life is unfair, suffering and death come to the just as well as the unjust. There is for him no life after death: 'All go unto one place, all are dust and all turn to dust again' (3.20). Old age will come and the last chapter contains a moving description of the failing faculties of old age: 'When men are afraid of a steep place and the song of the birds fall silent' (12.4). 'It is better to visit the house of mourning than the house of feasting' (7.2).

Ecclesiastes in the Hebrew bible

Ecclesiastes is a frank and honest book, comparable in its moving resignation with the Rubaiyat of Omar Khayyam. When the Jews made a list of their scriptures at Jamnia in AD 90 they nearly left it out and not surprisingly. It is as though we were to make a list of the devotional masterpieces of the twentieth century and alongside Dietrich Bonhoeffer's *Letters and Papers from prison* and William Temple's *Readings in St John's Gospel* we were to place Albert Camus' *The Outsider.*

The writer of Ecclesiastes wrestling with the apparent futility of human endeavour reminds me of Mr Prendergast in Evelyn Waugh's novel *Decline and Fall*. Mr Prendergast had been an Anglican clergyman until he had doubts; not trivial doubts about the validity of Anglican Orders but fundamental ones. 'I couldn't understand why God had made the world at all. Once granted the first step, everything else follows ... incarnation, church, bishops, incense, everything. But what I couldn't see and what I can't see now, is, why did it all begin?' So the writer of Ecclesiastes strikes a familiar chord. This is the world we know. Here are the questions which we ask and the answers which in our despairing moments we come up with.

Paul Tillich in his book *The Courage to Be*, suggests three main sorts of human anxiety, each characteristic of a period of history.[1] Anxiety about fate and death characterised the end of the ancient world; anxiety about guilt and condemnation was a mark of the medieval world. The modern world is concerned about emptiness and meaninglessness. Bertrand Russell describes human life as 'sitting on a narrow raft, illuminated by the flickering light of human comradeship, tossed for a brief hour on the rolling waves of the dark ocean.'

And yet I'm glad Ecclesiastes is in the Old Testament among the canonical scriptures. It serves two purposes: it keeps our religion honest and it inspires us to seek further.

Ecclesiastes keeps our religion honest

We sometimes conceal our real feelings, our doubts, scepticism and pessimism beneath a cloak of devotional rhetoric, ashamed to bring them to church with us. The Jerome Roman Catholic commentary says this about Ecclesiastes: 'The believing community sometimes creates the impression that all the faithful should be having a close personal experience of God and if they are not it is their own fault'. Do you I wonder feel guilty when the certainties, joys and triumphs expressed in our hymns, prayers and sermons do not resonate with you? The book of Ecclesiastes validates the day-to-day experience of many people. It reflects how life can seem to be for some people. And the writer's down to earth advice can provide consolation:

- Accept the ordinary joys God sees fit to give you;
- Do not long for the unattainable;
- Enter into life as it is with zest;
- Enjoy the good days and accept the evil days;
- Provide for the future.

These are prudential and limited objectives. The book of Ecclesiastes extends the scope of our religious experience to cover actuality. It broadens the horizons of our quest for meaning and roots our religious life firmly alongside the experience of our neighbours. The Old Testament scholar Robert Davidson writing about Ecclesiastes says: 'It is well to be reminded that faith is often hard won, for some impossible, and that joy needs to be tempered and deepened by the witness of the troubled mind'.[2]

Ecclesiastes encourages us to seek further

What is lacking in Ecclesiastes is the sense of pilgrimage, and the quest for God, which is a prominent feature of most of the books of the Old Testament. Let me suggest the early chapters of Genesis as an antidote to the pessimism of Ecclesiastes and indeed an answer to Mr Prendergast. Genesis begins with a collection of myths – creation, the fall, Cain and Abel, the flood and the tower of Babel for example – which explore some of the profoundest questions which human beings ask about life – its source, nature, and purpose and why God created us at all.

'The Lord God formed man... and breathed into his nostrils the breath of life', says the writer of Genesis. (2.7). The meaning of life lies here: in the uniqueness of human personality. In the mystery of human beings – in the bundle of emotions, will, thoughts, aspirations and sensations, there is an ultimate, something which needs no justification, which simply is. God made us to enjoy being us, realising the infinite creative possibilities which he has placed within us. To say that we are 'made in the image of God', is to say that God has planted in you and me a bit of the final secret of the universe.

But the writer of Genesis goes further and contributes a second justification. 'It is not good that the man should be alone. I will make him a helper as his partner' (Genesis 2.18). According to the poetic vision of Genesis God made Adam to be a companion for himself and Eve as a partner for Adam. The second thing which needs no justification is relationship. We are not made to be alone. In the infinite variety of human relationships – husband and wife, parent and child, brother and sister, boy and girl, friend and friend, man and man, woman and woman – is an irreducible experience, finally true and infinitely fulfilling. However full of tension relationships may be they are still the stuff of creation. So we hold together the two – our uniqueness and our relationships with the other.

These two very different Old Testament books, Ecclesiastes and Genesis, provide complementary insights into human life as it is. Ecclesiastes faces honestly the questions, which so many people ask about the meaning and purpose of human life. The author answers this realistically based on his experience. The early chapters of Genesis root the purpose of life firmly in the nature of God. It is his mysterious purpose to create human beings and to enable them to enjoy relationship with him and with each other.

1. Paul Tillich *The Courage to Be* Fontana 1962 c.2
2. Robert Davidson *The Old Testament* Hodder & Stoughton 1964 p.185

Parables of the Kingdom

What is a parable?

You were probably brought up, as I was, on a very simple definition of a parable: 'A parable is an earthly story with a heavenly meaning'. Here is a rather better one. It is by the great New Testament scholar and translator of the New English Bible, Professor C.H.Dodd. 'A parable is a metaphor or simile drawn from nature or common life, arresting the hearer by its vividness or strangeness and leaving the mind in sufficient doubt about its precise meaning to tease it into active thought'[1]. It doesn't, I'm afraid, trip off the tongue! P.G. Wodehouse has, in my view, a more memorable one. He it was, you will recall, who invented Jeeves and Bertie Wooster as well as Blandings Castle and the Drones Club. Here is his definition: 'A parable is one of those Bible stories that sounds a pleasant yarn but keeps something up its sleeve until the end and then pops out and knocks you flat.'

Parables in the teaching of Jesus

We all know that Jesus used parables a great deal in his teaching. Mark says 'Jesus never spoke to them except in parables' (4.34). The gospel reading frequently includes one or more of the parables of Jesus so this morning I want to speak about parables as a whole.

One third of all Jesus' teaching recorded in Matthew, Mark and Luke is in parables. There are in all about 60 parables in the gospels. Some are well known, fully developed stories like the Prodigal Son, the Good Samaritan, the Sower or the Labourers in the Vineyard. Others are brief one liners – 'No one after lighting a lamp puts it under the bushel basket, but on the lampstand, and it gives light to all in the house' (Matthew 5.15) Professor Dodd in his book The *Parables of the Kingdom*, said that nearly all the parables are about the Kingdom of God – they are about what it is like to acknowledge God's 'kingly rule' or His significance in our lives.

Why did Jesus make such frequent use of parables?

First of all, say the scholars, it was the method used by Jewish teachers, so Jesus was following the practice of the day. Second they say, he was for the most part talking to simple people who would neither understand nor remember if he taught them in abstractions. No doubt those reasons are correct. But there is a third and I think more important reason.

In 1967 the Canadian sociologist Marshall McLuhan published a book whose title became a catch phrase, *The Medium is the Message*. The media – television, radio, newspapers – he said, do not just report the news, they actually shape it. What you can get across is determined by the means you use. For example the tabloids and the broadsheet newspapers have the same sources but shape it so differently that you would never guess. Parables are an illustration of the same truth. They actually shape and determine the message itself. So the fact that Jesus uses parables so frequently tells us something about the Kingdom of God, about what he was trying to say to his disciples and to the crowds who came to listen to him. I want to suggest three characteristics of parables which are also characteristics of the Kingdom.

What does Jesus' use of parables tell us about the Kingdom?

Parables are down to earth – so is the Kingdom

Where do you think Jesus got his parables from? When I was learning to preach I was recommended to study a book by the great Methodist preacher Dr W.E.Sangster called *The Craft of Sermon Illustration*. Dr Sangster advised those who had to preach regularly to keep a card index of possible illustrations under appropriate headings. In the card index you should enter stories you heard, quotations from novels you read, anecdotes you came across, cuttings from newspapers, conversations with people and so on. They were all grist to the preacher's mill. It is excellent advice and probably essential if you are, as he was, preaching twice every Sunday in the same church to huge congregations.

I doubt however whether Jesus kept a card index from which he drew ideas for his next parable. As he went from village to village his parables were not pre-selected but grew spontaneously from the scenes he witnessed because to him the Kingdom had the immediacy of everyday experience. Everybody was talking about a house which had been swept away in a flash flood. A labourer had found some treasure trove so he had at once gone off and bought the field. There had been another nasty incident on the lonely Damascus road. At a wedding some of the bridesmaids had arrived late and so they were locked out. And each incident reminded Jesus of some aspect of the way God works in our lives.

The parables of Jesus were spur of the moment stories, they arose from the dilemmas, the crises, the opportunities of life, they were often about the frailties of human beings because Jesus wanted people to hear through these things the voice of God. They were about the nature of God's Kingdom. The experience of God's Kingdom is all of a piece with ordinary life –it feels like the joy of finding and buying a really beautiful and expensive pearl; it is like knowing that however hard the wind blows your house is secure. The Kingdom of God for us is to be found in the twists and turns of ordinary life, when relationships are rocky, when the college course is barren or when we have to work with somebody who is absolutely impossible.

Parables reverse human values – so does the Kingdom

Familiarity with the parables has blunted for us the strangeness, the paradoxes which many of them contain. Does God really prefer the spendthrift, greedy younger son who has gone off with the family inheritance to the dutiful elder brother? Would we really go out and collect tramps from the roadside and take them home for dinner? Surely we must sympathise with labourers who have worked all day and only get the same pay as those who put in an hour or so as it is getting dark.

There is no simple answer to any of these questions. You have to tease out the story and find what point Jesus is trying to drive home. But the strangeness of the parables reminds us that Christian faith is more than sanctified common sense. The values which Jesus taught are not identical with ours. God places a different valuation on money, reputation, social position and rank. The gospels make uncomfortably clear that Jesus had a bias for the poor, the rejected, the weak, the disadvantaged, the sick and the sinner. The Sermon on the Mount trips off our tongues and we forget how revolutionary is its message. 'The meek shall inherit the earth'; 'You will he happy if you are persecuted.' No surely not, not me anyway! The parables are about ordinary situations in life; they are stories which reverse our human values.

Parables call for a response – so does the Kingdom

Earlier I compared the parables of Jesus with sermon illustrations. But of course they are no such thing – they are the sermons themselves. At the end Jesus does not spell out the moral and tell the people what to do about it. He simply says 'He that has ears to hear let him hear'. Or to put it another way – What do you think? Go and work it out for yourself. Not surprisingly when Jesus has spoken there is often consternation, a buzz of surprise or even anger.

Jesus is not the sort of teacher who dictates notes, provides a blackboard summary, discourages questions in class, gives you a hand out or provides specimen answers to the questions which life poses. He simply tells a story – provoking, challenging, shocking, or even absurd and says, What do you make of that? And even more, What are you going to do about it? To put it in the modern jargon Jesus' teaching in his parables is interactive, resource-based learning. He is the sort of teacher who leaves the learning to you – he provides only clues for you to follow.

The parables of Jesus are not then just the way he taught about God's Kingdom but they capture the style of the Kingdom. It is a Kingdom which: touches the ordinary things of life; runs clean contrary to the ways of the world and demands our response in thought and action.

1. C.H.Dodd *The parables of the kingdom* Nisbet 1935 p.16

❧

The strange beginning of Matthew's gospel

Matthew 1.1–25

When I was about ten my godmother gave me a Bible for Christmas-Authorised Version of course. I was a precocious, serious-minded and, no doubt, repulsive ten year old and so on Boxing Day, instead of playing with my meccano, I sat down to read my new Bible. It was an odd book – floppy leather cover, small print, and between the two columns of text strange references. It was like no other book I possessed or had ever seen. I started at the beginning: 'To the most high and mighty prince, James '. Who, I wondered was he? Then I turned to 'The First Book of Moses, called Genesis'... I got as far as verse 22. 'Let fowl multiply in the earth, and the evening and the morning were the fifth day...' Then somebody told me that this was a book in two parts and that the second part was both shorter and easier than the first, so I found Matthew's gospel. This time I got only as far as verse 3. 'And Judas begat Phares and Zara of Thamar; and Phares begat Esrom; and Esrom begat Aram'. So on Boxing Day I went back to my meccano.

The gospel we have just read comes from the beginning of Matthew, not the family tree – no lectionary to my knowledge suggests that we should read that in church – but the next bit. I want however to speak about both the genealogy and about the passage we have just read. Both use the Greek word *genesis* though the English version conceals this by translating it in verse one as genealogy and in verse 18 as birth. In both Matthew is concerned with the origin or beginning of Jesus. I want to answer the question why Matthew begins his gospel like this and what it is he says to us about the origin of Jesus through this first chapter.

End and beginning

Let me start with a paradox: for Matthew the beginning is at the end. He is not interested in the conception, birth, childhood, or adolescence of Jesus for themselves. His focus, like all the gospel writers, is on Jesus' death and Resurrection. Each gospel has a detailed account of the events which led to the crucifixion and Resurrection. That for them is the beginning, the beginning of their Christian story, and the beginning of the life of the church. So the birth of Jesus is only significant on account of his death and Resurrection.

Let me illustrate. If you visit Blenheim Palace you will be shown the room in which Winston Churchill was born on 30th November 1874. There is a lock of his hair, his first rompers, photographs of his mother and father and so on. If he had died in March 1940 nobody would have been the slightest interested in his birth or childhood. It was the events of the Second World War, in which he became the saviour of the nation, which gave significance to his birth. The beginning is at the end.

So it is with Jesus. For each of the gospel writers the Resurrection matters most but in order to bring out who he was, each begins the story in his own way. So Mark begins with Jesus' baptism by John, Luke starts with the birth of John the Baptist, John gives us a chunk of theology and Matthew gives us a family tree and the story of Jesus' conception by the Holy Spirit. Let's turn then to Matthew. In chapter one he tells us two things: first that Jesus is the expected Messiah and second that he was conceived by the Holy Spirit. Let me say a little about each.

The expected Messiah

Matthew traces the family of Jesus right back to Abraham. It is not of course a factually accurate family tree – it couldn't be, the sources for compiling it didn't exist. It is a theologically inspired family tree. It is divided into three blocks each of 14 generations – from Abraham to David, David to the Exile and after the Exile. It ends with Joseph. Jesus, says Matthew, is at the peak and climax of Jewish history. He fulfils the hopes of the Jewish people. But the list is odd in a number of ways. It contains for example the names of just four women -Tamar, Rahab, Ruth and Bathsheba. All four are non-Israelites and all were prostitutes or had similar skeletons in their cupboards. So Jesus came not from a line of saints or supermen and women, not even from a pure Jewish line. He came from a family of ordinary human beings, including non-Jews and prostitutes. Jesus' heredity is not distinguished, sheltered, special and extraordinary. God uses very ordinary people to accomplish his will, some of whom may not even know they fit into his plan. And that goes for us too.

Matthew's family tree lights up the Old Testament for us and makes it indispensable reading for Christians. It makes sense of those wonderful passages, mostly in Isaiah, which we read during Advent and at the Christmas carol service. They are not prophecies of Jesus. Isaiah didn't know that centuries after his death Jesus would come along. What he did know was that God was leading his people out of darkness into light, out of despair into hope and out of war and strife into peace. And when Jesus came he fulfilled those hopes. It is Jesus who leads us out of darkness into light, out of despair into hope and out of war and strife into peace.

So says Matthew through that genealogy, Jesus is the Messiah in whom all the hopes and expectations of the Jewish people, expressed in the Old Testament, are realised in ways which they could not have imagined.

Conceived by the Holy Spirit

Second says Matthew in this opening chapter of his gospel Jesus was born to a virgin. The Virgin Birth is one of those doctrines with which some people have difficulty. It may have arisen we are told from a mistranslation of the word for young woman in Hebrew in Isaiah chapter 7. The Greek translation in Matthew is virgin. (compare Isaiah 7.14 and Matthew 1.23) Biologists have a problem with a mode of conception which runs contrary to all we now know about the processes of reproduction. Some feel it is odd to trace the ancestry of Jesus, as Matthew does to Joseph, if he was not his natural father. Others are concerned that a virgin birth might convey the impression that sex is somehow intrinsically unclean, unworthy of God's son. And if Jesus was a real human being then surely he must have had a normal human conception. What is more, outside the early chapters of Matthew and Luke there is no reference to a Virgin Birth.

There are of course arguments on the other side and plenty of Christians have no difficulty with the Virgin Birth. Let me therefore simply say that I think we should not question either the Christian commitment or the integrity of those who find the Virgin Birth a difficult doctrine to hold.

It is important to remember that Matthew's point is the specialness of Jesus. Jesus was, he says, conceived by the Holy Spirit. Well what does that mean? John Robinson who was Bishop of Woolwich in the 1960's wrote a short book called *But that I can't believe...* which consisted mostly of articles he had contributed to the *Sunday Mirror* and other tabloid newspapers, trying to convey in the simplest terms the basic truths of the Christian faith. He wrote this about the Virgin Birth.

> To say that new life was fathered and quickened in Mary by the Spirit of God is a profound way of expressing an inner truth about Jesus. It is to say that his birth and life cannot simply be thought of as biological events. ..He showed them a new kind of living, a new kind of loving quite out of this world. He seemed rooted in a security that couldn't be explained simply in terms of a human family background..[and he adds].. With regard to the biological details I am prepared to keep an open mind.[1]

'A new kind of living and a new kind of loving' – a way of living and loving not characteristic unfortunately of ordinary human beings, but evident in Jesus. Perhaps that helps us to understand something of what it might mean to say 'he was conceived by the Holy Spirit'.

So in that odd first chapter which caused such problems to a ten year old, Matthew tells us that Jesus is the Messiah so long expected by the Jewish people and that he was conceived by the Holy Spirit.

I want to finish this morning by offering you, for meditation and prayer, at the end of Advent and as we prepare for Christmas, some of the things which Matthew tells us about Jesus in this first chapter of his gospel.

- Matthew links Jesus with the hopes of Israel and with a human family. Christmas is the time when we connect with our past. We celebrate with our families, we remember those from whom we are separated, we recall those no longer with us, and we pray for the lonely.
- Matthew links Jesus with a wider family which includes some very odd people. We are part of a worldwide family of infinite variety to whom Jesus also came.
- Matthew reminds us that through Jesus God leads his people out of darkness into light, out of despair into hope and out of strife into peace. He leads us similarly this Christmas time.
- Matthew reminds us finally that God sent us his son to show us a new way of living and a new way of loving.

1. John A.T.Robinson *But that I can't believe* Fontana 1967 p.25

Thomas, the apostle

Blessed are those who have not seen and yet have come to believe. John 20.29

A few years ago the BBC ran a series of programmes called *Famous for Fifteen Minutes*. It consisted of interviews with people who had briefly come to public notice and equally suddenly returned to obscurity. There was you may recall Diana Gould, a housewife who challenged Mrs Thatcher on a phone-in programme about the sinking of the Argentinean warship, the General Belgrano; her persistence not to be crushed by the growing annoyance of the Prime Minister who was not used to being argued with let alone contradicted. Then there was Brian Taylor, head master of Kingswood Comprehensive School in Corby who flashed across the media firmament after a television series had for several weeks featured his school. He appeared on *Any Questions* before returning to obscurity.

Thomas in the gospels

Now Thomas was famous for an equally short time. We should scarcely have heard of him had he not been involved in the episode which we read in this morning's gospel. He is named in the list of the twelve apostles in Matthew (10.3), Mark (3.18), and Luke (6.15). He was not one of the leaders like Peter, James and John but among the also-rans about whom we know very little.

He was apparently a twin hence his name Didymus, the Greek for twin, a rather unimaginative nickname. Was the other twin a sister or a brother and was he or she a follower of Jesus? Before the incident recounted in John chapter 20 there are just two other scenes both in John's gospel in which Thomas makes an appearance. In the first (John 11.16) Jesus is going to Bethany where Lazarus lies dead. Thomas makes a remark which is hard to understand, 'Let us go as well so that we can die with him'; does it mean 'so that we can go to the funeral'? Later Thomas provides the lead in to one of Jesus' best-loved sayings. 'We don't know where you are going so how can we know the way?' says Thomas to which Jesus replies ' I am the way, the truth and the life'. (John 14.5-6)

Later legends

I'll come back to John chapter 20 in a moment. Let me finish the story of Thomas. He is to be found according to Luke with the other apostles in the

Upper Room after the Ascension, (Acts 1.13). After that he doesn't appear again in the New Testament. There is a legend that it was Thomas who took the gospel to India where he was martyred and buried at Mylapore, near the town of Chennai, though we probably know it as Madras. There you will find the Thomas stone erected in his memory dating from the seventh century. His body was, according to legend, subsequently brought back to southern Italy where it was reburied and a shrine erected at Ortona in the Abruzzi.

Thomas and the resurrection

Let me return to the incident which has made Thomas a household name. According to John's gospel Jesus appeared to his disciples behind locked doors on Easter evening. Thomas was not there. When next day he met the others the conversation went something like this:

> *Disciples* You'll never guess what happened last night. We saw Jesus.
> *Thomas* Go on. You're pulling my leg. You don't expect me to believe that. It must have been a ghost.
> *Disciples* No it was him. He showed us his hands and his side.
> *Thomas* (blustering) Unless I can put my fingers where the nails were; unless I put my hand in his side, I won't believe it.

A week later, the same place and once more the doors are locked. This time Thomas is there. Jesus offers the proof for which Thomas had asked.

> *Jesus* Put your finger where the nails were; put your hand in my side. Don't be unbelieving any more. Believe.

But Thomas does no such thing. The words of Jesus are enough and call forth from Thomas the words which are the climax of John's gospel: 'My lord and my God'. They constitute the last but one verse of the gospel. (Chapter 21 is a later addition)

> *Jesus* Because you have seen me you have found faith. Happy are those who never saw me, yet have found faith'.

These words have been described as the final Beatitude. Blessed, or perhaps Happy would be better, Happy are the meek... Happy are the pure in heart... Happy are the peacemakers.. and finally Happy are those who have *not* seen and yet have believed. That Beatitude represents the difference between those who had known Jesus in the flesh and later Christians whose belief must be based not on sight but on faith. John is writing some 60 years after the Resurrection, he is reflecting on the needs of Christians of his day. They were perhaps saying 'How can we know Jesus? It's all very well for you who knew him when he was alive'. John writes for them and for all subsequent generations of Christians.

Thomas and the faith of the church

We are in the same boat as Thomas and the hearers and readers of John's gospel. How we should like to see Jesus, to hear him, to touch him. You may recall the Victorian children's hymn which includes the lines '*I wish that his hands had been placed on my head, / That his arms had been thrown around me, /And that I might have seen his kind look when he said:/ Let the little ones come unto Me*'. But the nostalgia behind those words is precisely what Jesus is warning the disciples against. Our faith needs to be more robust. We cannot believe because our senses enable us to touch, hear and see. We can't put our fingers in the print of the nails, we can't hear his voice.

And yet we sometimes believe that in a rather different way we can still touch and feel. The Bible we think can provide us with first hand knowledge, we refer to it as the Word of God, an infallible means of encountering him telling us what to believe and how to behave. Fundamentalism it seems to me shows a lack of trust, a hankering after the kind of sense experience of the Thomas story. Some people fall back on the creeds and the teaching of the church or the Eucharist maybe to provide directions and unassailable contact with Jesus. All of them help us but none is a substitute for adult faith, believing without seeing.

Certainty is not the experience of most twenty first century Christians, neither clergy nor laity, bishops nor saints. John Habgood when he was Archbishop of York was once asked if he ever had doubts. 'Yes, often', he replied. 'When was the last time', asked his questioner. 'Yesterday morning', replied the Archbishop. I recently read the biography of Cardinal Hume written by Anthony Howard. In his epilogue he seeks to explain the remarkable appeal that Basil Hume had to so many people of his own church as well as those who were not Roman Catholics. He attributes it in part to the fact that he 'never shied away from admitting that he, too, was no stranger to the kingdom of doubt'.[1] Doubt then is not a form of unbelief but part of the experience of faith and it is reflected in the Bible. 'O that I knew where I might find him', says Job (23.3). 'My God my God why have you forsaken me' says Jesus on the Cross, quoting Psalm 22. (v.1) 'Truly you are a God who hides himself ', says Isaiah (45.15).

Father Kelly the Mirfield Father once said 'The opposite of faith is not doubt but certainty'. To live by faith is to live with uncertainty. We shall come alongside the interested enquirer, the person with a tentative, questioning faith when we are prepared to share our own vulnerability, to admit our own questions and doubts.

The Biblical post-Resurrection faith is that of Thomas who believed even though he had not seen. William Temple concludes his commentary on this passage with a quotation from the First Letter of Peter: 'Whom, not having seen, ye love; on whom, though now ye see him not, yet believing, ye rejoice greatly with joy unspeakable and full of glory' (1.8 AV)

1. Anthony Howard *Basil Hume, the Monk Cardinal* Headline 2005 p. 316

The great feast

Luke 14.1–24

How to be a guest and a host

Luke often uses meals as a setting for discussion and debate. Meals were an indication of status – who you invited, where they sat in relation to each other and even the quality of the food you served were all expressions of status. We can easily identify with these concerns because we do the same.

Here in chapter 14 Luke uses an episode at a Pharisee's dinner party as the setting for sayings of Jesus which are all about entertaining friends. First he records two pieces of advice Jesus gives, the first to guests and the second to hosts. He tells guests invited to a marriage banquet not to head for the top table even if that is where they think they are entitled to sit, in case somebody even more important turns up and they lose face by having to find a seat lower down the table. And he tells anybody giving a dinner party not to invite their friends and neighbours because they will only invite them back on the dinner party circuit but instead to invite the poor, the maimed, the blind and the lame, and the reason – because they can't return the invitation. But as consolation he adds, 'You will be repaid at the Resurrection.'

The dinner party

You can imagine the frisson of shock and horror which would have run round the table. Jesus then endorses and underlines the second piece of advice with a story about a man who is giving a dinner party which he has planned weeks ahead. The day before the party he picks up the telephone, 'You haven't forgotten have you?' He gets a similar reply from each of the guests: 'I'm terribly sorry I shan't be able to come after all'.. And out come the excuses – 'I've bought a field – only time I can go and check it out' … 'I've bought ten oxen, I've just got to make sure I haven't been done'…. 'I've just got married – she won't let me come – you do understand don't you?'. Each excuse must have brought a smile to the face of the hearers.

What should the host do? Call the party off and change the date. No, says Jesus, withdraw the invitations and instead invite the poor, the crippled, the lame and the blind. Luke comments 'Not one of those who were invited shall come'. What an unlikely tale.

The Messianic banquet

Jesus apparently told the parable after one of the guests had said, 'Blessed is anyone who will eat bread in the Kingdom of God'. The Jews believed that they had been invited to the Messianic banquet where they would meet Abraham, Isaac, Jacob and the prophets. It would be confined to Jews; there would be no Gentiles there. But says Luke, the Jews have already said no to John the Baptist, they had by the time he wrote refused to recognise Jesus for the person Christians believed him to be, so God will fill up the places at the Messianic banquet with those previously rejected – the Gentiles. He won't be spurned, he won't cancel the banquet, he will instead extend the invitation. The parable is about the inclusiveness of the Kingdom of God. It is all of apiece with the whole thrust of Luke's gospel. He alone of the gospel writers for example includes the Magnificat: 'He has brought down the powerful from their thrones, and lifted up the lowly; he has filled the hungry with good things and the sent the rich away empty.' (1.52-53)

The peril of exclusiveness

Exclusiveness is not confined to the Jews of the first century, it is a human characteristic. We all naturally prefer in-groups, people like ourselves, people whose life-style and interests we share. All very natural, but not Christian. Part of the stumbling block of the gospel is that it will have nothing of exclusiveness. The church is for all, the Kingdom is for all, the gospel is for all. What a platitude, until you begin to unpack it. Not for WASPS (White, Anglo-Saxon Protestants) alone; not for Anglicans alone; not for the middle classes alone; not for those of high IQ and a good education; not even for the virtuous, and the good living. It is an uncomfortable but unavoidable truth. Here are three examples of those often not invited to our twenty first century feasts.

Who are excluded?

The Two-Thirds World

A few years ago I was a member of a party from the Bishops' Waltham deanery which went to the diocese of Calabar in Nigeria as part of IDWAL (the Inter-Diocesan West African Link). I was privileged to preach in Calabar cathedral and I did so on this passage in Luke, though it was a rather different sermon from this one. The congregation was unforgettable. In front of me were some 400 people, many of them young, between 18 and 30. Most of them were among those excluded humanly speaking from the banquet. Some were unemployed and some lived in houses which lacked the basic amenities of life which we take for granted. Their education had often been brief, interrupted or abruptly terminated when the money gave out. Some had lost members of their families prematurely because medical treatment was not available. Some were the victims of a tyrannical and corrupt regime. In Lagos we had seen even more spectacular examples of the underprivileged, some living in cardboard cities, scavenging for scraps on rubbish heaps, washing their babies in puddles in the streets.

I came from a country whose people had for many years had the opportunity to come to the banquet but I was in a country many of whose citizens had hitherto been excluded. The issues are complex but the principle is clear. People from the Two Thirds World are included by God in his banquet. We must exemplify that in the way we behave towards them. The cancellation of Third World debt is just one way this can be expressed.

Some social groups

In the Kairos process which all the churches in the Portsmouth diocese are undertaking we have been asked to think the unthinkable. I wonder if one of the things which should cross our minds is the lesson of this parable. How can we open the church not just to our social circle, those who understand our liturgy, enjoy our worship, and join our house groups, the sort of people who have for generations been the backbone of the Church of England. How can we be open to those who come only for a wedding or a funeral? How can we welcome those who come on Remembrance Sunday or to Communion on Christmas Eve? And what about those who never even think of approaching a church at all? If a wider social spectrum is to be attracted to church how should we change to make them feel at home? Would the style or even the times of our services have to change? What about how the PCC does its business? How about the range of our activities? Is the church really for all? We were asked recently to undertake a SWOT analysis (strengths, weaknesses, opportunities and threats). Some members of our congregation identified a degree of complacency as one of the threats – a bold conclusion and an uncomfortable one.

Gay people

In 1997 the bishops of the Church of England asked us all to listen to the experiences of gay people so that we should have some idea of the discrimination which many of them suffered and of what their sexuality meant to them. On the whole the church has not done so though we at St Peter's have done more than most. Of course gay people are welcome – as long as they repent, as long as they keep quiet about it, as long as they remain celibate, as long as they don't ask the church to bless their partnership, as long as they don't seek ordination. But perhaps they too are people whom Jesus invites to the Messianic banquet on equal terms with all the others who will be there.

This parable, like so many of the others that Jesus told, was an arresting and disturbing one to all who heard it. Let me finish with an illustration. On 22nd June 1948 *The Empire Windrush* docked at Tilbury bringing almost 500 West Indians to the British Isles which they regarded as their mother country. It was the beginning of a substantial immigration from the Commonwealth. Many of those who came were Christians as a result of the missionary activity of the British churches. They expected a warm welcome from their fellow Christians which sadly they did not always receive. I recall one powerful image which appeared years later on television. A black man from the Caribbean attended an Anglican church in London for some weeks. He was the only black person in the congregation but he persisted. One Sunday after the service the Vicar approached him. The congregation he said was uncomfortable as a result of his presence; they felt he didn't fit their church. Would he, said the Vicar, please find another church to attend?

Jesus said 'When you give a banquet, invite the poor, the crippled, the lame and the blind and you will be blessed.' Luke 14.14

Labourers in the vineyard

I choose to give to this last as I give to you. Matthew 20.14

The parables of Jesus are among the most memorable passages in the Bible. They are not however as straightforward as they look. We need amongst other things to know about the first century Jewish background against which they are set. They have been misunderstood and trivialised over many centuries. The parable of the talents is not for example about using our abilities to best effect. It is addressed to Jewish leaders who had buried the revelation which God had given them and refused to share with other races. The Good Samaritan is not about doing good turns when you can but about the limits of law and the demands of love. It too contains an implied rebuke to the Jewish leaders – the man who fell among thieves was rescued by a Samaritan, amongst the most despised of races.

A baffling story

The parable in today's gospel reading is both among the best known and also the most baffling. If you have been on holiday in a Mediterranean country – France, Spain, Greece or Italy for example – and seen hills covered with vines laden with ripening grapes, you will be able to imagine the scene. It is very important to harvest the grapes at exactly the right moment if you are to use them to make the wine you want. It must be neither too early nor too late.

So the owner of this vineyard has watched the grapes ripening as well as keeping an eye on the weather. One morning he concludes that conditions are right to harvest his grapes. He hires labourers and agrees to pay them a denarius, the accepted amount for a day's work, enough to live on but not much more. Later in the morning the weather still looks good, there are plenty of men in the market place looking for work so he takes on another shift and makes the same agreement with them. In the early afternoon, the hottest part of the day, he does the same and again an hour before dusk he takes on yet more workers. There are still plenty of grapes and plenty of labourers wanting jobs it seems.

As dusk falls the day's labour is over and the men stop work. The steward pays them all the agreed rate. Surprisingly the last to be hired are paid first and are amazed to receive a full day's pay. Those who have worked all day naturally expect proportionately more and are angry that for their long and exhausting day's labour they receive exactly the same as those who have scarcely worked up a good sweat. There is no bonus for unsocial hours and no overtime payment.

You don't need much imagination to visualise the scene. There is consternation, and uproar as the union representative gets in touch with the local secretary of the Grape Gatherers Union. There are threats of sympathetic strikes. The television cameras arrive. Politicians of all parties are invited to comment and each points out that their party will amend the law to stop such a thing happening again. I must curb my imagination!

Some interpretations

Why did Jesus tell such a strange and apparently provocative story? What can it possibly mean? A well-known American preacher said in a sermon on the parable: 'We cannot read it without seeing the finger of Jesus probing beneath the surface of the vast realm of business'. Perhaps it is an attack on the work shy, or a commentary on the indifference of a government to the unemployed or even a demand for a national minimum wage. Is it a call for socialism or a defence of capitalism? It is of course none of these.

The generosity of the kingdom

At the beginning of the parable Matthew quotes Jesus' words: 'For the Kingdom of Heaven is like a landowner who...' It is a parable about the Kingdom of God. It is about God and his attitude to men and women not about employers and their attitude to their employees – the Kingdom of God not the kingdom of business.

The key is to be found in verse 14, in Jesus' words to one of the complainants: 'I choose to give to this last as I give to you'. It is about the generosity of the employer whom Matthew describes as *kurios,* the Greek word for Lord. It is about the generosity of God who gives to all equally not because we've earned it or deserved it. The pay the employer gives is not related to need, to the hours worked, or the quantity of grapes picked but simply because he chooses. That is the sort of person God is. To belong to his kingdom is to recognise that.

Let me give you an imperfect analogy. You decide to give presents to three people. One is your mother, a second is a friend who has been ill and the third is the child of a neighbour whom you scarcely know but who has few friends. You do not weigh up what each deserves, the closeness of the relationship, or how much they may spend on a present for you when your birthday comes along. What you give is your decision; it is an expression of your generosity, your love, and your concern in each case. You don't calculate what each deserves. You don't tell each of them what you have given to the others.

That says Matthew is what God is like. The parable is part of his controversy with the Pharisees who felt entitled to special rewards when compared with those usually bracketed together as 'publicans and sinners'. The Kingdom of God is an undeserved gift. The labourers hired last felt a sense of gratitude which was a corrective to the corrosion of envy, resentment, bitterness and rivalry. In a sense we are all labourers who have come on the scene at the end of the day. We all receive more than we deserve.

Experiencing the generosity of the kingdom

Let me finish with an illustration and two quotations. Ian Ramsey who was Bishop of Durham sadly died in 1972 at the age of 57. He was a distinguished philosopher of religion and was often spoken of as a future Archbishop of Canterbury. In March 1934 when he was an undergraduate he contracted tuberculosis, at that time a life–threatening illness. He spent some time in a sanatorium at Papworth near Cambridge. He regarded his recovery from tuberculosis as a sign of the Kingdom and he resolved to be ordained. He was a remarkably accessible person with the common touch and a distinct northern accent. A friend wrote after his death that his inability to say no to any invitation to speak for a cause in which he believed almost certainly hastened his death: 'It was as though his life, unexpectedly put in jeopardy, had been restored to him and had become a gift which he must ever after use as completely as he was able'.

The first quotation is from T.W.Manson, a great New Testament scholar of the mid-twentieth century who comments on the story as follows: ' It is fortunate for most of us that God has not dealt with us on the basis of strict justice and sound economics ... There is such a thing as a half part of a denarius ... it is called a *pondion*. But there is no such thing as a *pondion* of God's love, no such thing as a half of God's love'.

The second quotation is from a hymn by Charles Wesley:

> Thy ceaseless, unexhausted love,
> Unmerited and free ...
> Its streams the whole creation reach,
> So plenteous is the store,
> Enough for all, enough for each,
> Enough for evermore. [1]

1. *Hymns and Psalms* Methodist Publishing House 1983 48 vv.1 & 4

Jerusalem or Athens?

Acts 17.22-31

The city of Athens

Athens is an incomparably beautiful city. In the first century, long before urban sprawl and pollution occurred, it must have been even more beautiful. The city is dominated by the Acropolis, a rock which rises sheer to over 500 feet, crowned by the Parthenon, a temple dedicated to the goddess Athena, the protector of the city. It was built in the fifth century BC and in Paul's time had not been damaged by Turkish gunpowder. This was the city of Socrates, Plato and Aristotle. By the time of Paul's visit on his second missionary journey in AD 51 its great days were over but it still prided itself on its sophistication and intellectual tradition. Paul spoke to the crowd on the Areopagus, a hill close to the Acropolis. Today the marble surface has been worn to the smoothness of glass by generations of tourists but it still commands a wonderful view over the city.

Paul's address

Paul's speech is more like an address delivered at Speakers' Corner in Hyde Park than a sermon in Westminster Abbey. It is wholly unlike any other address recorded in the New Testament whether delivered by Paul or anybody else.

Paul's first sermon recorded in Acts chapter 13 was addressed to the Jews in the synagogue at Antioch. Speaking to people who knew the Old Testament, he started with Exodus, summarised Jewish history and showed how the death and resurrection of Jesus was its fulfilment. And that is the pattern of all the other sermons recorded in Acts – except this one. In Athens Paul was speaking to a completely different audience: to non-Jews, to people who acknowledged a whole host of gods and goddesses. There were shrines to them all over the Graeco-Roman world.

When Paul was invited to address the crowd on the Areopagus he did not so much as mention Jesus. He started where they were, not by denouncing the inadequacy of their gods but by establishing a point of contact. 'As I came along I noticed', he says, 'an altar to an Unknown God. What you worship as unknown, that I proclaim to you.' And he goes on, 'God is not far from each one of us, for in him we live and move and have our being. God gives to all, mortal life and breath and all things' (vv.27-28). In saying this he is quoting a sixth century poet Epimenides, then well known, just as a preacher today might quote Shakespeare or Wordsworth. So Paul took their superstitions, their half-formed beliefs, and the insights of their poets as the starting point of his address.

Two assessments of Paul's address

Now some people say that at Athens Paul made the mistake of his life, one which he recognised and which he never repeated. Instead of preaching Christ he watered down his message, he preached natural religion, something which, say the critics, never saved anyone. As one church historian of the early twentieth century puts it, 'Did any so-called apology for the faith make a Christian?' But, say the critics, Paul learnt his lesson. He went on from Athens to Corinth and in his first letter to the Corinthians, he was perhaps reflecting on his experience at Athens when he wrote: 'For I decided to know nothing among you except Jesus Christ and him crucified …My speech and my proclamation were not with plausible words of wisdom … so that your faith might rest not on human wisdom but on the power of God'. (1 Corinthians 2.1–2.)

Let me however put an alternative view. Paul's address at Athens has also been called 'a model of missionary tactics', 'how to proclaim the gospel to an unfamiliar audience', how to connect with people who can make nothing of Jesus Christ as the saviour of the world.

Making contact

All of us are aware how difficult it seems to have become to establish a point of contact between the gospel and our neighbours. If you hear an open air evangelist for example I wonder if your reaction is like mine – to wonder what chords his words are striking in the minds of his hearers, what contact does he have with shoppers going about their business.

And yet the pollsters tell us that 70% of people claim to believe in God. Their God however is the Unknown God, not the God of full blown Christian belief, not the God of our hymns, readings and creeds, not the God of the institutional church with which they are unfamiliar or disenchanted. There is a vast gulf between the 70% who claim to believe in God and the roughly 5% who attend church regularly. It is these with whom we need somehow to connect. Perhaps at Athens Paul showed us a way.

Paul's address is a model of an alternative way to make contact. We must not denounce the inadequacy of what people believe, we must not scoff at the vagueness of their convictions, we must not dismiss natural religion. We must offer a point of contact and try to open new horizons, draw on human experiences which we all share. 'The God who made the world and every thing in it.... He made all nations so that they would search for God and grope after him and perhaps find him, though he is not far from each one of us. In him we live and move and have our being' (17. 24,26-28). Paul's words would describe the beliefs of many of the 70%.

Experiencing the unknown god

People may indeed grope after God deep in their own experience. They may not *speak* of God at all. They may describe instead a sense of longing; they may be moved by the beauty of nature; they may speak of depth, incompleteness, of unaccountable joy, of an experience which takes them beyond themselves, a profound awareness of the sacredness of other people, of experiences which make them feel more fully human. They may not put such feelings into words at all but still experience them. These are the raw materials for deeper belief, for further searching. And these are experiences which we share, which are common to all of us.

A Methodist minister David Deeks writes, in a book entitled *Calling, God?* about what he calls indicator experiences – the sense of awe, of moral demand, of self-identity, of angry compassion. 'In each of them, he says, we find our minds, our wills and affections directed to something outside ourselves, an indication of a reality beyond and beneath our normal everyday life'. [1]

When I was an Ofsted inspector visiting secondary schools we were required to assess how far the school contributed to spiritual development of pupils. We used to ask facetiously 'Who's doing awe and wonder this week' – and often it was me! It was made clear to us that we should look for spiritual awareness not just in religious education lessons or in school assembly but, for example, in the quality of relationships between staff and pupils and between pupils themselves, in the way in which science was taught so as to lead to a sense of wonder at the marvels of the natural world and at how far music and art lifted pupils beyond their ordinary day to day experience into the spiritual. We noted displays of pupil work in classrooms enabling them to show creativity and originality. Even history, geography or mathematics could be the means of educating for spiritual awareness. Spiritual development came for many children through natural religion, rather than the conventional routes of Christian prayer and worship.

And these experiences of depth can occur in the most unlikely places. Richard Holloway, the former Primus of the Scottish Episcopal Church describes a visit to Sissinghurst, the garden created by Harold Nicholson and Vita Sackville-West, where in the White Garden he had a religious experience of great intensity. 'It was', he says, 'as if someone beyond this world was seeking to communicate with me through this world'.

Experiences of the God within may come to us not only through beauty and goodness but sometimes through pain and suffering. A woman who had suffered from a cancer recalled the experience on a radio programme and said ' I wouldn't have missed the experience. I have never felt so near to God'. The German theologian Jurgen Moltmann was converted to the Christian faith in a German concentration during the Second World War. He wrote subsequently 'The experience of misery and forsakenness and daily humiliation gradually built up into an experience of God'.

When Paul addressed the Athenians he spoke of the Unknown God, the God shared by Christians and non-Christians alike, experience of whom comes to us because we are human beings, from deep within as well as from outside ourselves because He made us. Paul sought common ground with his audience and he found it in natural religion. It is an approach which we should consider. We have I believe in the church undervalued natural religion. We have lost contact with the religious experience of a great many people; we do not sufficiently value experience of the God in whom we live and move and have our being. We do not often enough celebrate in our worship the experiences of depth, awe and wonder, moments of disclosure which connect us with the religious awareness of human kind.

Some people see Jerusalem and Athens, revealed religion and natural religion, Cross and Resurrection and the Unknown God as opposed to one another. But they are complementary; the Cross and Resurrection through the Unknown God; not Jerusalem or Athens but Jerusalem through Athens.

1. David Deeks *Calling, God?* Epworth 1976 pp 9-11

Introducing Paul's letter to the Romans

The letter to the Romans in church history

The year is 386 AD the place a garden in Milan. Augustine, a man of 32, not yet a Christian, is sitting with a Bible at his side when an angel appears; *Tolle, lege -(Take up and read)* says the angel (speaking in Latin as all angels did until Vatican II when the pope gave them permission to speak in English!). So Augustine takes up the Bible and reads from Paul's letter to the Romans: 'Put on the Lord Jesus Christ, and make no provision for the flesh to gratify its desires' (13.14). It was the turning point of his life; the following Easter he was baptised and became the most influential Christian after St Paul in the first 1000 years of the church.

Move on 1150 years. The place is Germany. Another man in his early thirties is struggling to find peace with God. Martin Luther too discovers, to his immense relief, through studying Paul's letter to the Romans, that we are saved not by what we do but by what God has done for us in Christ. Luther was to describe Romans as 'The chief book in the New Testament and the purest gospel.'

Two hundred years later and we are in London in May 1738. An Anglican clergyman, another man in his thirties describes in his Journal a key religious experience. He went to a meeting in Aldersgate Street 'where one was reading Luther's *Preface to the Epistle to the Romans*. About a quarter before nine ... I felt my heart strangely warmed. I felt I did trust in Christ, Christ alone for salvation...'[1] The man was of course John Wesley, the main figure in the evangelical revival of the eighteenth century.

Today's New Testament reading is the first of a series from Paul's letter to the Romans, so I want this morning to introduce this great letter. I want too to urge you to read it yourself, not just the brief snippets set in the lectionary but right through. But let me at once put the health warning on the packet – this is not an easy read, for reasons which I will say more about later.

The background to the letter to the Romans

The letter to the Romans was written in 57 AD – that is about 25 years after the Crucifixion and Resurrection and probably ten years before Mark, the earliest gospel. Paul wrote it while he was in Corinth at the end of his third missionary journey. He had been a Christian for 20 years so this letter is the fruit not of youthful enthusiasm but of mature, Christian experience.

It is Paul's longest letter and unlike his others it is not concerned with internal crises in any of the churches which he had founded or visited. He had never been to Rome. It is more a manifesto than a letter. It may even have been a circular letter which was adapted for each of the churches to which it was sent.

Paul's gospel

Well what is its central theme? It has been described as the fifth gospel, the gospel according to Paul. The others- Matthew, Mark, Luke and John – tell us about the life, ministry, suffering, death and Resurrection of Jesus. That is their way of proclaiming the good news. Paul is not concerned with the birth, life and ministry of Jesus at all; he never mentions them. He is concerned exclusively with Jesus' death and Resurrection. Paul's gospel hinges on the significance for him and for all Christians of those two events.

His gospel arises from his own personal experience. About three years after the Resurrection he had met Jesus on the Damascus road. He regarded that meeting as equal to the Resurrection appearances to the disciples: 'Last of all he appeared to me also' (1 Corinthians 15.8) he writes. From that moment his life was centred on Christ. To use a phrase which Paul employs again and again to describe Christians, he was 'in Christ.' 'If any one is in Christ there is a new creation, everything old has passed away and every-thing has become new', he writes to the Corinthians reflecting his own experience. (2 Corinthians 5.17)

But Paul remained a Jew and so he is deeply exercised about the relation between the Christian faith and Jewish law. The gospel, he is sure, is for Jews even though to his profound sorrow most of them have not accepted Christ as the Messiah. But there were also Gentiles in the church at Rome and Paul knows there is a place for them too. Romans shows him wrestling with the place of both Jews and Gentiles in God's plan.

Paul's achievement in the letter to the Romans is to bring together his passionate conviction, his personal experience of Christ and show how it works and what it means; what God was doing when he allowed Jesus to suffer on the Cross and when he raised him from the dead and how it affects us. Romans is the theology of a converted man. Here is one of the ablest minds in the early church wrestling with his own experience and putting a rationale on it. It is hard to think what Christianity would be without Paul and without this book. A medieval churchman, Anselm, talked of ' Faith seeking understanding'. Paul in Romans is doing precisely that – trying to understand and communicate to others what God has done for him and potentially therefore for all people.

Let me come back however to the health warning. This is not an easy book to read. It is sometimes inconsistent or downright contradictory. The thought world is unfamiliar and some of the ideas are obscure. Paul some-times loses himself in the complexity of his own argument. I often think that if he had known that we should be reading it 2000 years later he would have tried harder to make his meaning clear and perhaps redrafted some of the more abstruse parts!

Let me also say that what we have in the letter to the Romans as in the rest of the New Testament is an account of the faith of a first century Christian not a twentieth century Christian. We have to reinterpret that faith to meet our own situation. We cannot simply read off what we should believe about everything from what Paul tells us. Paul's views on women, slavery, authority, sexuality, cannot simply be swallowed whole. They arise from his own experience and relate to the thought world of the first century. They have to be thought through in relation to our culture and our lives.

The message of Romans

Let me finally attempt to summarise the message of Romans. It is no less than to answer the question, What is Christianity? Paul starts where we are: his intuition and experience tell him that, on their own, human beings are never righteous and cannot put themselves right with God. He spells this out in the first three chapters of the book. 'All have sinned and come short of the glory of God' (3.23). He goes on to apply it to himself: 'I can will what is right, but I cannot do it' (7.18 b). And the consequence of that is clear: 'Wretched man that I am who will rescue me from this body of death?' (7.24) He realises that only God can save. His grace comes from outside ourselves as an undeserved gift for us to receive. The word grace occurs over 20 times in Romans.

And the result is an immense sense of relief, release and peace: 'Since we are justified by faith, we have peace with God through our Lord Jesus Christ, through whom we have received access to this grace in which we stand'. (5.1–2) ' For the law of the Spirit of life in Christ Jesus has set me free from the law of sin and death' (8.2). Once saved we can never be separated from the love of God. ' I am convinced that neither death nor life ...things present or things to come... or anything else in all creation will be able to separate us from the love of God in Christ Jesus our Lord' (8.38-39).

This immense sense of gratitude results in a different sort of living. 'Present your bodies as a living sacrifice, holy and acceptable to God, which is your spiritual worship'. (12.1) And so in the last chapters Paul spells out the behaviour required of a Christian, based not on obligation or commandment but on gratitude, our response to the grace of God. Such a brief summary cannot begin to do justice to this great book. I can do no more than urge you once more to read and wrestle with it as so many Christians have done in the past.

Later in the service we shall sing the hymn which begins And *can it be that I should gain an interest in the Saviour's blood....* I have chosen it not just because it is by the greatest hymn writer in the English language – though it is! – but for two other reasons. Like all Charles Wesley's hymns it is a mosaic of scriptural quotations and it breathes the atmosphere of the letter to the Romans. ('The range of theology has rarely been equalled in one hymn' says one writer.) [3] But second it conveys the sense of wonder felt by Wesley as also by Luther and Augustine as they lived the Christian life. And that sense of wonder they received at least in part through Paul's letter to the Romans. It is a sense of wonder much more difficult to experience in the hard faced, sophisticated, secular twenty first century. It is nonetheless authentic Christianity.

1 *The Journal of John Wesley, a selection* Oxford University Press 1987 pp.34-35
2 *Common Worship Lectionary Year A* Principal service Propers 4-19
3 *Companion to Hymns and Psalms* Methodist Publishing House 1988 p.152

Introducing Ephesians

Not a letter, not by Paul, not to the Ephesians ?

One of the advantages of the *Common Worship* lectionary is that it provides readings on consecutive Sundays from the same book of the Bible. Today's New Testament reading is the first of a series of seven from the letter to the Ephesians. So this morning, I want to offer you an introduction to this important book.

Important yes, but not perhaps as straightforward as it may appear. Ephesians is *not* really a letter, it is probably *not* by Paul and it was *not* addressed to the church at Ephesus! Needless to say scholars disagree about these matters. (Disagreement is as essential to scholars as bread is to a baker – without it he or she would be unemployed!) So don't let's worry if there isn't scholarly agreement about Ephesians.

Let me however rehearse the arguments briefly. According to the Acts of the Apostles Paul spent three years in Ephesus so he must have known many of the Christians there yet Ephesians contains no personal greetings. There are no references to the specific conditions of the church at Ephesus. The name of Ephesus in chapter 1 verse 1 is not found in the earliest and best manuscripts. The vocabulary and style are different from Paul's letters. In some important ways the theology is different too: there is strong emphasis on the church and it is no longer the local church meeting in people's houses but the universal church.

Highlights of Ephesians

But none of that – questions of authorship, who it was addressed to or whether it is a letter – detracts from the value of Ephesians for Christians today. It remains one of the greatest books in the New Testament.

- It contains one of the most profound prayers ever written (3.14-21). It begins, 'For this reason I bow my knees before the father, from whom every family in heaven and on earth is named ...'
- It sets out how Christians are to conduct controversy in that often quoted phrase 'speaking the truth in love' (4.15).
- It describes the mysterious powers of evil in the world against which Christians have to strive as ' the principalities and powers, the rulers of the darkness of this world' (6.12 AV).
- It tells us that in this battle we are equipped with 'the whole armour of God: with the belt of truth, the breastplate of righteousness, the shield of faith, the helmet of salvation, and the sword of the Spirit'. (6.10–17)
- It includes the great clarion call to unity in the church 'There is one body and one Spirit... one Lord, one faith, one baptism, one God and Father of all, who is above all and through all and in all...' (4.4-6)

I must in all honesty add that Ephesians also contains that contentious section with which over half of you are likely to disagree: 'For the husband is the head of the wife just as Christ is head of the church... wives be subject to your husbands as you are to the Lord' (5.22-24) It is a passage which is not surprisingly usually omitted from lectionary readings.

The structure of Ephesians

Well what is the nature of this important book? First date. We are no longer in the heady days after Pentecost, nor even the heroic age of Paul's missionary journeys. Paul has been dead for some time – perhaps as much as 30 years. It is the end of the first century; the church is 60 years old.

Second its nature. Ephesians is less a letter than a manifesto or a circular letter, intended for the many churches established round the shores of the Mediterranean, summarising the essentials of Christian faith and life. The sender perhaps filled in the name of each addressee in the greeting at the beginning as we use our computers to create the illusion that a circular letter is in fact a personal one.

Third content. Like other New Testament letters it falls into two parts: chapters 1–3 are theology and chapters 4-6 are practical – how Christians must live as a consequence of what God has done for them. 'I therefore, the prisoner of the lord, beg you to live a life worthy of the calling to which you have been called' ...(4.1) But the theology is never theoretical or abstract. The author is so overwhelmed with what God has done, with the message he has to communicate that the only language in which he can convey it is that of prayer.

Through the first three chapters there runs a mood of prayer. In chapter one a single prayer of thanksgiving runs from verse 3 to verse 14 and resumes in verses 17 to 19: In chapter 3 verse 14 the author bursts into prayer once more: 'For this reason I bow my knees before the father...' So the theology of chapters one to three is expressed in the language of wonder and surprise at what God has done. I once heard a sermon at All Souls, Langham Place by John Stott, the noted evangelical preacher, on a verse in Romans in which he repeated again and again the phrase: Doxology precedes theology. Praise, prayer, worship are paramount and are the natural result of contemplating God's revelation.

A summary of the theology of Ephesians

Let me try and summarise what calls forth this wonder. 'God' says the author, 'is the one Father of us all'. He intends us to be his sons and daughters. But the world has a great tragedy at its heart, which affects not only human beings who 'are dead through trespasses and sins' (2.1) but also the whole world, which disrupts God's intended plan. That tragedy is something which only God can put right from outside and he has done so through what the writer calls 'the mystery of Christ'. 'The mystery of Christ' and 'the wisdom of God' are key phrases in this book (for example 3.4). 'He is rich in mercy... he made us alive together with Christ.'

God's plan then is to restore the whole human race, not just Jews but Gentiles too. Gentiles were, he says, once aliens, strangers, without Christ but now they are included. The greatest divide in the ancient world, that between Jews and Gentiles has been bridged. 'Christ is our peace, he has broken down the dividing wall. He has made us one new humanity in place of two' (2.14). God brings harmony between himself and humankind and so makes possible unity between humans themselves.

But second he has created a new body to exemplify this unity, harmony and reconciliation – the church. The writer calls it 'the household of God', ' a holy temple', 'the bride of Christ', the place where God lives in the world. It is built on the apostles and prophets and Jesus Christ is the cornerstone (2.19-22). The church is a beacon for the world, the evidence for the work of unity which God has accomplished. The church is the focus of Ephesians as it is for no other book of the New Testament.

God's intention and the real world

Well that, much simplified and in a nutshell, is the message of Ephesians chapters 1– 3. It is like a great symphony with the same themes appearing but with variations. No wonder the writer was moved to praise and prayer. But how does it relate to us and to the world in which we live? A few weeks ago the Rector referred in a sermon to the doctrine of double agency used to account for the gulf between the world as God intended it to be and the world as we experience it. Here in Ephesians is an example of something very similar. The writer is overwhelmed by what God has done through Christ in breaking down the barriers between himself and humanity and between human beings themselves and so building a new community in the church. But of course he doesn't force it on us; we remain free to frustrate his plan, to nullify what he has done. And there is plenty of evidence that we have done just that and gone on doing it.

So this book holds up the world as it might be, humanity as it could be and the church as it should be. The Christian faith is potentially revolutionary: imagine a world patterned as God intended. We have to hold together the world God intended and the world humanity has created. As Christians we strive for God's world and God's church. We strive to bring peace, to break down barriers between rich and poor, black and white, man and woman, gay and straight, between Christian and Jew, Hindu and Moslem, because in God's intention we are one humanity through 'the mystery of Christ'. And the same goes for the church; that too is one in God's plan and when we strive to make it so we do his will. Here then in this great New Testament book is a vision to inspire and hard truths to challenge us in our life in the church and in the world.

A plea – read Ephesians as a whole

I suggested at the beginning that it is an advantage of the new lectionary that we read from the same book of the Bible on consecutive Sundays. The advantage is I'm afraid illusory. Not many of us can guarantee to be in church on seven consecutive Sundays. And if we are how many of us will be saying to ourselves 'Ah yes I remember what he or she said last week, I really can't wait for the next instalment'. The truth is that we don't read any other book, whether it is a novel or a computer manual, like that – in small gobbets at weekly intervals.

So I want to conclude by asking you to read Ephesians, not once but several times in the next few weeks, until you are familiar with it. And read it in a modern translation, not the King James' version. The King James' version may contain beautiful prose but its vocabulary is complex and some of its sentences are interminable – one in the first chapter of Ephesians has over 200 words (vv.15-23).

David Ford is Regius Professor of Divinity at Cambridge. He is neither a priest nor a minister but a Reader in the diocese of Ely. He writes this: 'After ten years of trying to plumb the depths of Ephesians I feel I have only distilled a few precious drops of its extraordinary daring truth; but how intoxicating.' I have found something similar reading and re -reading Ephesians in recent weeks.

JOHANNINE SIGNS

Water into wine

Out of his full store have we all received grace upon grace for while the law was given by Moses grace and truth came through Jesus Christ. John 1.16-17

A few years ago *The New Statesman* ran a competition which required you to write a publisher's rejection slip for a book which subsequently became famous. You might for example explain why *Robinson Crusoe, Tale of Two Cities* or *Harry Potter* were rejected. The winning entry was about *St John's gospel*. It ran like this: 'There are already three versions of this well-known story in circulation; a fourth version is unlikely to gain market share. We recommend rejection'.

We all know that John's gospel was published and has been a best seller ever since. For many people it is perhaps their favourite gospel. It contains so many well known verses – 'God so loved the world that he gave his only begotten son...(3.16) 'In my father's house are many dwelling places' (14.2) 'I am the way, the truth and the life' (14.6) 'I am the resurrection and the life' (11.25) Only in John's gospel do we find the account of the feet washing which we enact on Maundy Thursday.

It is in many ways different from the first three gospels. It has for example no account of the birth of Jesus but instead opens with those profound words, 'In the beginning was the word, and the word was with God ...'(1.1). It contains no account of the Temptations, the Transfiguration or the Last Supper. There are far fewer short sayings of Jesus and more long speeches attributed to him. The early part of the gospel contains accounts of what the writer of John calls signs. In fact the first twelve chapters of John have been described as 'the book of signs'. I want this morning to talk about the first sign – described in chapter 2 – the turning of water into wine.

Jesus attends a wedding at Cana

On the face of it the incident in which Jesus turns water into wine is a simple story. Jesus with his mother and brothers are guests at a wedding in the village of Cana not far from their home in the village of Nazareth. It is a happy occasion as weddings usually are and there is plenty to eat and drink. Before the reception is over however the waiters report that the wine has run out. His mother draws Jesus' attention to the problem. He in turn tells the waiters to fill six stone jars, each of which would hold about 20 or 30 gallons, with water to the brim. They are to draw off the water and take it to the steward who didn't apparently know that the wine had run out. The steward comments on the quality of the wine in the jars and remarks that it is a novelty to save the best wine to last rather than serving it first as was the usual practice.

Some strange features

It is not however quite as simple a story as it might appear.

- There are the curious words spoken by Jesus to his mother when she points out that the wine has run out: 'Your concern is not mine. My hour has not yet come'. The commentators have had a field day with that and there is much ingenious exegesis.
- Then there is the sheer volume of the wine. Jesus appears to have turned between 120 and 180 gallons of water into wine. Hostile critics have called it ' a miracle of luxury'. Would it have been sensible to provide a further 120 gallons or more when everybody had already had plenty to drink. The needs which Jesus usually met were for the sick, the blind or the disabled. More wine for a party where there had already been plenty seems out of character. He doesn't so much meet a need as supply an extravagance.
- Then there are the words 'On the third day' – a phrase which is usually a pointer to something especially significant.
- Why six stone jars? They are a symbolic reminder of the Jewish rite of purification.
- There is no account of what must have been a spectacular incident in any of the other gospels.
- And finally the incident seems to run counter to Jesus' rejection of miracle as a way of reaching people.

The first 'sign'

And yet this story has been described as, 'the key to the whole gospel'. The clue, say the commentators, is in the words in verse 11:' Jesus did the first of his signs in Cana of Galilee and revealed his glory, and his disciples believed in him'. The incident is described as a 'sign', a word which John uses in his gospel where the other gospel writers use the word 'miracle'. A sign is a story whose significance is far deeper than outward appearances, 'a visible pointer to the invisible truth about the person who performed it'. It is more than a pledge or token; it is an external event which conveys an internal truth.

What then is the invisible truth about Jesus to which this incident is a pointer? Jesus was born into the Jewish faith and so were his mother and the disciples. Judaism was to them infinitely precious. It had a great past; it had been the vehicle through which God had revealed himself to his people throughout their turbulent history and through the great prophets. For Christians it was however no longer sufficient to reveal God fully. Now it had run out as surely as the wine at the wedding feast. Many of its leaders and in particular the Pharisees had turned it into a series of legal requirements. It no longer gave life. It failed to convey a living experience of God. The old wine had run out.

What is to replace Judaism? The answer was the new wine of the gospel and in particular the man who made wine out of water in the purification jars. John the Baptist is recorded in the previous chapter as saying: 'The law came through Moses, grace and truth through Jesus Christ' (John 1.17). And some of the other features of the story convey the same truth. The huge quantity of wine, between 120 and 180 gallons, stands for 'the sheer inexhaustible abundance of grace' – 'out of his full store have we all received grace upon grace'. (John 1.16) And, say the commentators, this explains the curious words which Jesus apparently addressed to his mother 'Your concern is not mine. My hour has not yet come'. Even Mary represents Judaism, Jesus was born into it but when his hour comes – the hour of Crucifixion and Resurrection – he will transcend Judaism.

Water into wine

The signs in John's gospel are not just tales of long ago but a proclamation of the gospel for today. For the early Christians they were not simply stories of spectacular doings attributed to Jesus. They were illustrations of what the Risen Lord was able to do in the church of their day. And the miracle has gone on being re-enacted in the history of the church and in individual lives ever since. Water is turned into wine, gospel grace is rediscovered, and new life brings freedom and release.

The miracle of water into wine is the story of church history, the renewal again and again by the miracle of turning the water of legalism into the wine of the gospel.

In the twelfth century the Cistercian Order broke through the aridity of the old monastic rule – new wine to replace wine that had run out. In the thirteenth century St Francis attracted people by his simple life style when the church it seemed had begun to atrophy. In the sixteenth century Luther and Calvin freed the church from a religion which had become legalistic, corrupt and dead with the new wine of the gospel. In the eighteenth century John Wesley and the evangelicals released new energy to a church in which the gospel had been replaced by a dry conformism; once more water was turned into wine.

But sometimes the reverse has happened. The church itself has allowed the wine to run out and water has replaced it. It was the nineteenth century Danish philosopher Soren Kierkegaard who once said 'Christ turned water into wine but the church has succeeded in doing something even more difficult. It has turned wine into water.' How vigilant we must be that we do not in our generation do something similar – quenching the wine of the gospel.

The meaning of this first of Jesus' signs is that the law given by Moses – the Old Testament dispensation – has run out and the new dispensation is nothing less than the new wine of the gospel, exemplified by Jesus himself.

'*The law was given by Moses, grace and truth came through Jesus Christ*'.

Feeding five thousand

John 6.1–14

A modernist interpretation

Modernism is the name of a movement in theology in the first half of the twentieth century which tried to relate the Christian faith and the Bible to modern thought and in particular the findings of science. It raised questions about how we should understand the miracle stories of the New Testament in the light of scientific knowledge about matter. How could Jesus turn water into wine, raise Lazarus from the dead or walk on water?

I first encountered modernism, though not of course the name, in a divinity lesson (what we now call RE or RS) when I was an eleven year old in my first year at grammar school. Our divinity master was the local congregational minister whose war work was to become a school master in addition to his church work. We studied the New Testament and reached the Feeding of the 5000. He asked us what we thought happened. We were non-plussed so he told us what he thought happened. Many of those in the crowd round Jesus, he said, had brought their lunch with them though some hadn't. The personality of Jesus so impressed the crowd that those who had brought their sandwiches spontaneously shared them with those who hadn't, so that all had plenty to eat and there was lots over. So, said my divinity master, the miracle was not Jesus multiplying food but turning selfish people into people who cared and shared to meet the needs of all. Our homework was to explain what we thought happened. I was not a rebel and in any case I thought his explanation was very ingenious so I wrote it out in the green ink which I then preferred and got 10/10!

A prominent story in all four gospels

Today I would not take the same view. The Feeding of the 5000 is still a perplexing story. Yet we can't dismiss it as peripheral. It is the only story which appears in all four gospels. In fact there are six accounts of apparently miraculous feeding in the gospels. (Matthew 14.13-22 & 15.32-39, Mark 6. 32-45 & 8.1–10, Luke 9.10–17, John 6.1–14) Mark and Matthew each have two. On one occasion Jesus feeds 5000 people, with five loaves and two fishes and there are twelve baskets over. On the second occasion he feeds 4000 people with seven loaves and a few fish and there are seven baskets over. John's account includes some details which do not appear in the other three gospels. John tells us that it is Passover time. He says that Jesus asks Andrew where they can buy bread for all to eat and Andrew draws attention to a boy who has five barley loaves and two fish. John it appears heightens the miraculous element in the incident.

Our interest is naturally in what happened; how did he do it? Let me say straight away that the text does not say that Jesus multiplied the food, though it is an implication from what follows. There are however problems about a literal interpretation. The people express no surprise at what happened. And in addition Jesus seems to have set his face against becoming known as a miracle worker. The truth is that we shall never know what happened. Like so many stories in the New Testament we can only wonder. There are two further questions, however, which are far more important. What was the significance of the Feeding of the Five Thousand for the writer of the gospel and for his hearers? And second what is its significance for us?

The new Moses and the new Elisha

This story is one of the signs which figure prominently in the first part of John's gospel. John highlights this story because it revealed who Jesus was. In verse 14 he says 'When the people saw the sign Jesus had performed the word went round, Surely this must be the prophet that was to come into the world'. When the Messiah came the Jews believed he would be a new

Moses and a new Elisha so they expected him to do what Moses and Elisha had done. When the Israelites were wandering in the wilderness Moses had fed them with manna. (Exodus 16. 13-26) So when Jesus fed the 5000 they said 'Here is the new Moses' – the Messiah has come, Elisha had fed 100 men with 20 barley loaves (2 Kings 4. 42-44). So when Jesus fed the crowds they said 'Here is the new Elisha'. So the interest of the gospel writers and the early church is not in what happened or how he did it but on what the story told them about him. He was Messiah and this story confirmed this conviction.

The Eucharist

By the time the gospels were written Christians were meeting on the Lord's Day to share a meal which Paul describes in his first letter to the Corinthians and which originates from the meal which Jesus took with his disciples on the night before he died (1 Corinthians 11. 23-26). What Jesus did when he fed the 5000 is strikingly reminiscent of what he is described as doing at the Last Supper and what we do when we take part in the Eucharist. He *took* the loaves and fishes from the boy, he *gave thanks* to God, he *broke* them (though John's account doesn't include the breaking) and he *distributed* them to those who were seated. All six accounts of the feeding in the gospels include the four actions (except the omission of the breaking by John). So commentators make a link between the Feeding of the 5000 and the Eucharist. But that does not exhaust its meaning.

Later in the same chapter of John's gospel Jesus gives his teaching on the Bread of Life which provides a devotional commentary on the story. 'I am the bread of life. Whoever comes to me will never be hungry and whoever believes in me will never be thirsty' (v.35) 'I am the living bread that comes down from heaven. Whoever eats of this bread will live for ever. (v.51) The bread which is Christ is not confined to the Eucharist. He provides the necessities of life. As one preacher commented 'Jesus never said I am the cake of life'. No 'I am the *bread* of life', that without which we cannot be adequately nourished.

More symbolism

But even that does not exhaust the symbolism of the story. What about the twelve baskets over – the inexhaustible food available like the manna in the wilderness – the food that is apparently not diminished by eating it – the food made for a needy world available because we have eaten and want to share it?

There is too the symbolism of the different accounts of the feeding. The Feeding of the 5000 we are told is symbolic of the Jewish world – the five loaves stand for the five books of the law and the twelve baskets over for the twelve tribes. And the Feeding of the 4000 stands for the gentile world. The seven loaves and the seven baskets over, stand for the seventy nations of the gentile world. The gospel is for both Jews and Gentiles.

Significance of the sign

The signs in John's gospel are not then accounts of past events performed by an itinerant wonder worker. They are illustrations of what the Risen Christ was doing in the church to which the gospel was addressed and is doing in the church today. He is still taking the loaves and fishes – the things we have to offer. He gives thanks over them. He breaks them and distributes them for the life of the world. The emphasis falls on how he feeds us in our daily pilgrimage. In the words of the great Welsh hymn, Guide me O thou great redeemer, *Bread of heaven, feed me now and ever more.*

6♪

The raising of Lazarus

Jesus said I am the Resurrection and the life. John 11.25

There are two ways to read a detective story. The usual way is to start at the beginning. In chapter one the scene is set for the crime – a country house party, a lonely farm or the Orient Express. In chapter two the murder takes place. In chapter three the local policeman appears, a bumbling yokel licking his pencil and laboriously taking statements. In chapter four the amateur sleuth enters. He or she unravels the crime with smooth efficiency and in the last chapter, to your surprise, your favourite character is revealed as a villain, the obvious crook throughout. If only you had followed the skilfully planted clues.

The less usual way of reading a detective story is to start with the last chapter. Here Hercule Poirot assembles the suspects, Lord Peter Wimsey explains the clues or if you are a devotee of P.D. James' Inspector Dalgleish solves the mystery. Then you go back to the beginning and of course, because you know who 'dun it', you don't miss any of the clues.

Now the gospels are detective stories which need to be read in this second way. The clues are to be found in Matthew 28, Mark 16, Luke 24 and John 20 & 21. It is the Resurrection which provides the clue to all the rest. The reason is that the gospels are not just about the man Jesus of Nazareth. They are about the Risen Christ who lived in the daily experience of the Christian church. The gospels were written to enrich their understanding of faith in him, a faith which is the result of the Resurrection. An under-standing of who he was requires the Resurrection.

The sixth sign: the raising of Lazarus

The story of the raising of Lazarus, part of which we have just read, is told in great detail. It consists of no less than 44 verses. Let me remind you that one of the ways in which John's gospel differs from the other three is that in the early chapters the author describes six 'signs', supernatural events whose significance lie not in the events themselves but in what they say about the person who performed them. In each case the miraculous element in the story is heightened so that it is inescapable.

- At the wedding feast at Cana Jesus makes at least 100 gallons of wine. (2.1–11)
- He heals the royal official's son without going to his bedside. (4.46-54)
- The paralysed man lying by the pool hasn't walked for 38 years. (5.2-9)
- Jesus feeds no less than 5000 people. (6.4-13)
- The blind man whom Jesus heals has been blind from birth. (9.1–7)
- And this last sign the raising of Lazarus is the most spectacular of all because when Jesus raises him Lazarus has been dead for four days and has already been buried. (11.1–44)

Did Jesus physically raise Lazarus?

The question which any twenty first century person is bound to ask is did it happen? Can we really believe that Jesus restored to life somebody who had been dead for four days? It contradicts all we know about the process of death. If blood ceases to flow to the brain for even a few seconds there is irreparable brain damage. What is more if Jesus really did raise Lazarus why don't Mark and the other gospel writers mention it? The trouble is that if you say, 'No, Jesus didn't raise Lazarus', you are accused of scepticism and if you say, 'Yes, he did', you are guilty of credulity.

Did Jesus literally raise Lazarus is a natural question for anybody to ask but it is not one in which the New Testament shows any interest. The story is told in such a way as to answer quite a different question: not did Jesus raise Lazarus but does Jesus raise us? Let's go back to the detective story. This is a question which requires the insight of the last chapter of the gospel, the account of Jesus' own Resurrection, to answer.

The impact of the story

The story of Lazarus as John tells it contains a great deal of fascinating detail.

- When Martha and Mary first tell Jesus of Lazarus' illness he says: 'This illness does not lead to death; rather it is for God's glory so that the son of man may be glorified through it'(v.4). And he waits two days before he goes to Bethany where Lazarus is.
- When Jesus hears that Lazarus is dead he says 'I am glad I was not there so that you may believe. But let us go to him' (v.15).
- When he gets there Lazarus has been dead for four days and Jesus says; 'I am the resurrection and the life. Those who believe in me even though they die will live, and everyone who lives and believes in me will never die'(v.25).
- And finally when Jesus raises Lazarus he says 'Unbind him and let him go'(v.44), suggesting triumph over the power that held him bound.

The cumulative impact of the story is not on the fact of the raising of Lazarus but on the motive for doing it. Running through the whole story and the detail it contains is the conviction that it is Christ the Messiah who is acting and that what he is doing is a present reality for Christians as individuals and as a community. He is making a new humanity; he is raising people from death. John's signs are ways of proclaiming what he can and is doing for people.

- If they are blind to the realities of life he is opening their eyes.
- If they are paralysed with fear then he is releasing them.
- If they are hungry then he is giving them the bread of life.
- If they are disabled he is putting them on their feet again.
- If they are dead he is raising them to new life.

In all these ways he is restoring men and women to life, acting on their whole personality, giving them the new life which only he can make available. The transition from death to life will take place not at some remote last day or even when we die but when we hear his voice and claim the new life he offers. The transference of future to present, of the end to now, is the essence of Jesus' teaching about the resurrection and the life.

The Lazarus experience

The Christian life then is a Resurrection. 'If you have been raised with Christ, seek the things that are above.' says the writer of Colossians in the passage which we read on Easter Day (3.1). In effect what Paul says is 'Haven't you had a Lazarus experience?' Haven't you proved the truth of 'I am the Resurrection and I am the life? So the raising of Lazarus poses for us the question: How would *you* live if you had been raised from the dead?

SPECIAL OCCASIONS

Remembrance [1]

There is a time for silence Ecclesiastes 3.7

On this first Remembrance Sunday of the twenty first century it is inevitable that we should look back on the whole of the twentieth century – a century unparalleled in human history for the scale of brutality, human suffering, death and destruction.

In the perspective of history we now see the First World War, not as an isolated episode, still less as ' the war to end all wars' but the key to the rest of the century, the beginning of a world wide conflict whose repercussions have extended over all the years since and include conflicts still going on. All are part of a vast human tragedy. The First World War left eight and a half million combatants dead, the Second World War over 14 million combatants and a further 27 million civilians killed and that does not count six million victims of the Holocaust.[2] Such figures defy all analysis or imagination. Not since the Black Death in the fourteenth century has death so uniformly affected every village and town in the British Isles and much of Europe.

It is scarcely surprising that we are still traumatised by the sheer scale of such death and destruction. No week goes by without another portrayal of some aspect of the wars of the twentieth century on television and radio. The grieving continues and will last well into the twenty first century and it is that of which this Remembrance service forms part.

How then are we to respond as we look back, on this first Remembrance Sunday of a new century? People have tried over the years to do it justice in words: in novels, plays, memoirs, poetry, as well as in painting and music. I think of John Singer Sargent's huge canvas in the Imperial War Museum entitled *Gassed*, with blinded soldiers each with his hands on the shoulders of the man in front, of Benjamin Britten's *War Requiem*, R.C.Sherriff's play *Journey's End*, the poetry of Wilfred Owen, Siegfried Sassoon and many others.

But no painting, no music, no words however eloquent can plumb the depths of so great a tragedy. In the words of the writer of the book of Ecclesiastes, *There is a time for silence*. Silence is the keynote of remembrance – the silence observed this morning at the Cenotaph in Whitehall, the silence which forms a central part of this service and all others held in churches and in the open air today, the silence which has been reinstated at the eleventh hour of the eleventh day of the eleventh month and was observed throughout the country yesterday.

But what sort of silence shall it be? The silence of emptiness – of wondering when it will end, or the silence of grief and nostalgia maybe? I want to suggest a threefold silence – the silence of recollection, the silence of reconciliation and the silence of resolve.

The silence of recollection

Those millions who died, servicemen and women, and civilians, of all colours, creeds and countries, are too vast to visualise. What we can do is to particularise, to visualise our own dead. We owe an enormous debt of gratitude to Keith Harrington who has so painstakingly researched the details of those from this village who died in the two wars and whose Book of Remembrance we shall soon be able to see and read.[3] There are 35 names on the war memorial. Len Horner who died in 1994 at age of 97 once told me that he knew every single one. They had been his contemporaries at the village school, in the Scout troop, the football team and the church choir. In the First World War the great majority of villagers died on the western front and are buried in cemeteries in France and Belgium. Six served in the navy and are buried at sea whilst one is buried in Jerusalem. Four lie in the Swanmore churchyard.

Ernest Targett is just one of those who died in France. He was a teacher at the school from 1908, Scoutmaster, gifted musician, occasional church organist and bandmaster at Knowle hospital. Until his marriage he lived just across the road from the church. He joined up in March 1916 and was killed near Ypres eighteen months later at the age of 31. Jack Hoar a loyal Old Swanmorian, who had known him as teacher, scoutmaster and friend, told me over 60 years later with tears in his eyes that he would never forget him. But it was not only those who were killed in the war. As you came into church this morning you passed the grave of Arthur Southwell who died in 1928, as the inscription says 'After ten years of suffering caused by the Great War'. The sons of two successive Vicars were killed and are commemorated on plaques in church. In the south aisle is a window dedicated to three brothers of the Gunner family who all died in the war.

Of the 13 from Swanmore who died in the Second World War four were in the Royal Navy, two in the Merchant Navy and one was a Royal Marine who died a prisoner of war in Crete. Of the remainder three died at El Alamein, Casino and Bayeux and the other three lie in our churchyard. The victims of both wars left behind widows and orphans, sorrowing mothers and fathers, brothers and sisters, boy friends and girl friends.

Try then to recollect in the silence real people, people known to you by a faded photograph, a pile of old letters or a collection of war medals. If we can let's, even at this distance in time, put a name and a face to our remembering. And where we do not know names let's enter into each other's recollections so that our silence is a vivid and real one.

The silence of reconciliation

Over the years remembrance has changed; it has become quieter, more reflective, less triumphalist and jingoistic. We are far enough away to acknowledge that wars are rarely the exclusive responsibility of one side. Even the Second World War, rightly laid mainly at the feet of Adolf Hitler, had other contributory causes – a vindictive peace treaty after the first World War, the economic collapse of Europe, the facile pacifism of the 1930s and the well intentioned but weak appeasement of French and British politicians.

Nor is suffering the monopoly of one side – Remembrance brings us closer to those who once were our enemies. Archbishop Robert Runcie was surely right when he insisted that at the service at the end of the Falklands War in 1982 we should remember the dead and bereaved of Argentina as well as our own, that the keynote should be reconciliation not triumphalism.

We no longer believe, as our war memorials suggest that God is exclusively on one side – ours. 'For God and the Fatherland ' is inscribed indiscriminately on the memorials of both sides – Britain, France and Russia but no less of Germany, Italy and Turkey. The God and Father of our Lord Jesus Christ is not in the pockets of any one nation. If we listened he would have uncomfortable things to say to us all.

We are more realistic too about the dead. We used to use elevated and heroic language to describe all who fought whether as conscripts or volunteers. There were of course heroes; those who rescued wounded comrades at risk to their own lives; those who faced torture rather than betray a friend; those who remained at their post even when they were badly wounded. But the vast majority on both sides did their duty, died not willingly but because they were where the shell landed, in the house the bomb struck, on the convoy that was torpedoed, in the plane hit by enemy flak. So remembrance will contribute to mutual understanding, to compassion, to drawing us together – to the silence of reconciliation.

The silence of resolve

No remembrance is worthwhile if it is only about the past. It must be about the present and the future. Many will recall Leonard Cheshire, who won the

VC for exploits as a pilot in the Second World War. He was as a result chosen to witness the dropping of the first atomic bomb on Hiroshima in August 1945. His response was to dedicate the rest of his life to the relief of suffering. When he died a few years ago he left behind a chain of Cheshire Homes all over the world to provide relief for the terminally ill with cancer.

Many of you will remember Ron Paterson who was Vicar here for 23 years from 1962-1985. It was his experiences as a serving officer in the navy in the Second World War culminating as Beach master on D Day which led him after the war to leave the navy and train for the Anglican priesthood.

Schools now often include a visit to the cemeteries, museums and monuments of the First World War in their history syllabuses. History becomes not a string of names and dates but an opportunity to learn from the terrible experiences of the twentieth century. I have heard pupils describe how they had seen the Menin Gate, the memorial to 55,000 allied soldiers with no known grave in Ypres and been moved to tears. A Cambridge undergraduate after a similar visit wrote in her college magazine. 'The tour ended at a German cemetery headed by two statues – one of a father, one of a mother, kneeling before their lost son. The tombstones of the dead soldiers lay before them. Already for me the tour had changed from a study trip into a pilgrimage – something I felt I owed it both to myself and to the 1914 generation to do.... For the first time on the trip it began to rain. Water began to stream down the sides of the statue. Soon the mother would begin to cry.'[4] The final test of our remembrance is how we live tomorrow. The silence of resolve.

Hiroshima

Let me conclude by recalling perhaps the most poignant silence I have ever experienced. In December 1989 I visited Hiroshima, the Japanese city on which the first atomic bomb was dropped on 6th August 1945. It is a bustling, modern, industrial city rebuilt after the war but the area devastated by the atomic bomb has been set aside as a permanent memorial. At its centre is Peace Park with countless monuments of great beauty and haunting power. The most moving experience for me however was walking round the huge museum filled with images of unforgettable poignancy. People of many nations were there. Nobody uttered a word; we walked round in total silence.

This experience brought together for me the three silences about which I have spoken.

- *The silence of recollection* – the images of destruction were there for all to see; the radiation for example which etched the outline of bodies on the pavement.

- *The silence of reconciliation* – there was no sense whatever that this was a Japanese memorial. It was about human beings locked mutely together in tragedy.
- *The silence of resolve* – in the book of Remembrance in the Peace Museum, Hiroshima somebody had written 'We shall not repeat the evil'.

There is a time to keep silence.

1. Sermon at the Remembrance service at St Barnabas', Swanmore on 12th November 2000
2. Figures are taken from Norman Davies *Europe, a history* OUP 1996 pp.1328-29
3. Details from *The Swanmore Book of Remembrance*
4. *Emmanuel College Magazine* (Cambridge) Volume LXXV 1992-1993 p.51

Bell-ringers' Sunday [1]

A multiplicity of bells,
A changing cadence, rich and deep,
Swung from those pinnacles on high
To fill the trees and flood the sky
And rock the sailing clouds to sleep.

In country churches old and pale
I hear the changes smoothly rung
And watch the coloured sallies fly
From rugged hands to rafters high
As round and back the bells are swung.

You may recognise those lines. They come from John Betjeman's *Church of England thoughts on hearing the bells of Magdalen Tower, Oxford*. They capture something of the thrill many of us experience when we hear the bells of St Peter's ringing out over the village or across the surrounding fields, particularly on such evocative occasions as a frosty Christmas Eve or a sunny May morning.

Yet church bells are not at the heart of church life. The vital furniture of worship includes the altar, the lectern, the pulpit and the font, the chalice and paten. These symbolise the essence of our worship through word and sacrament. The bells are a bonus, an optional extra, a plus not a necessity. No Methodist or United Reformed church, and few Roman Catholic churches have a peal of bells. It is unlikely that a new church of any denomination will ever again have the luxury of a peal of bells. When a church was built in the neighbouring village of Swanmore in 1845 all that it needed was a single bell in a small turret at the west end to remind villagers that it was time to come to church. Only in the 1870s when St Barnabas' was going up in the world was a bell tower added with a peal of six bells.

There is a further problem for a preacher on Bell-ringers' Sunday – the Bible has little to say about bells. According to Psalm 150, trumpet, lute and harp, tambourine, strings and pipe and clanging cymbals are the instruments with which we are to praise God in his sanctuary. No mention of bells. Bells appear only twice in the Bible. In Exodus chapter 39 verse 25 we are told: *They made bells of pure gold and put the bells between the pomegranates on the lower hem of the priest's robe as the Lord had commanded Moses.* (I haven't checked to see whether the hem of the Rector's alb is adorned with bells and pomegranates!) The second reference is in the book of Zechariah chapter 14 verse 20: *There shall be inscribed on the bells of the horses Holy to the Lord.* Neither text offers much scope for even the most imaginative exegesis.

What then shall the preacher say on Bell-ringers' Sunday? I want to suggest that the bells stand for two things. First, for the continuity of faith, worship and church life. Second, for the link between church and community.

Continuity of faith, worship and church life

There has been a church on this site for over 850 years. The present bell tower was built a mere 500 years ago. The parish records, which date from 1538, tell us that on 31st December 1582 the tower collapsed. It was rebuilt and the earliest of our bells was cast in 1597 too late to warn of the approach of the Armada or to celebrate its defeat. Our youngest bell was cast in 1937 to commemorate the recently ended reign of King George V.

If you visit the ringing chamber you will see reminders of its history. There is for example a verse of admonition dated 1766 about the behaviour which was expected of the ringers.

> You Ringers all that use this Belfry
> Your Hats throw off your Gloves lay by.
> The Steward's fees you can't deny.

And if a bell you overthrow
You shall pay two pence ere you go.
And if you take God's name in vain
You shall pay sixpence for your Pain.
And if you shall a Wager lay
Or such a thing presume to say
You shall for that a penny pay
And when you come the Bells to ring
Drink soberly. God save the King.

So ringers – take off your hat and gloves, no blasphemy, no gambling, no visit to *The Bunch of Grapes* on the way to church.

But there is much more to remind us of the long continuity of faith and worship. There is a board commemorating the peal rung over a century ago on 22nd January 1903 to mark the accession of King Edward VII, as well as that rung on 31st December 1999 to welcome the new Millennium.

You will find too the chart used by the Local Defence Volunteers – later renamed the Home Guard – to identify enemy aircraft – Junkers, Messerschmitts and FokkeWulfs – in the Second World War.

The bells then have been rung across the village for over 500 years, heard by men and women who have long ago been laid to rest in the churchyard. The bells were rung to mark events secular as well as sacred – to celebrate victory, to mark the passing of a monarch and to proclaim a new one, to mark births, marriages and deaths. The passing bell was rung well into the twentieth century, and indicated the age and sex of the deceased. The bells remind us that faith and secular life have been intertwined for as long as England has been Christian.

Link between church and community

Second, the bells represent the continuing link between church and community. It is surely symbolic that you can enter the tower without coming into church. A relatively small proportion of those who live in Bishop's Waltham are today regular worshippers at St Peter's but all hear the bells. They are a tangible link between the church and the community, a reminder that the boundary between faith and community is blurred.

The bells stand for the public declaration that we are here to proclaim the Kingdom of God, that all life is enriched and sanctified by the Christian presence, that the values of faith, hope and love are for all. The bells remind us that the values we proclaim in church have universal currency and that the goals we pursue are ones we share with people of all faiths and none.

They are values we share with social workers, doctors and teachers; they are the goals which should inspire our economic and political life. They are values and goals which we share with our neighbours – truth, integrity, support for each other in times of crisis, giving a helping hand.

But I want to extend the metaphor. The bells are rung in church and heard outside. But we need to be people who not only speak to the world but also listen to what the world is saying to us. Let me give you three examples.

First, on the last weekend in May [2003] the leaders of the world's richest nations met at Evian in France. The summit was intended to focus global attention on Africa. My newspaper devoted the whole of its front page to a statistical comparison between life in the G8 countries and the African continent. The disparity was stark and the statistics deeply disturbing. There is only time to give you a few examples. Access to clean water – 100% in the developed world; 45% in Congo: annual spending on health – in Canada $2534 in Mali $1: number of people per doctor – in Italy 169; in Malawi 50,000: number of people in Africa living on a dollar a day 291 million: average annual income – in the developed world $28,000, in Africa $1,690 and so on. The bells speak to me of a world out there of which we are a part, for whose exploitation we must share responsibility and justice for which we must strive.

Second, a few weeks ago I went to an exhibition at Tate Modern Gallery on the South Bank in London. It was called *Cruel and Tender* and subtitled *The real in 20th century photography*. It explored the realist tradition in twentieth century photography. It avoided nostalgia, romanticism, and sentimentality in favour of clear-eyed observation. It set out to record what is never hidden but rarely noticed. It included portraits of Somali women and Afghan refugees. There were concrete walls and buildings devoid of human presence and much, much more. It was for me a profoundly religious experience. It reminded me of the extent of human suffering but also the extent of human courage and resilience. It reminded me too that the raw material of prayer, worship and meditation is to be found not only in *Common Worship*, the hymn book and in volumes of prayers but in the world around us, in its poetry, its television and its photography. The world speaks to us through culture and mass media.

My third example is rather different. We need to hear what the world is saying to the church. In May [2003] Canon Jeffrey John was nominated Suffragan Bishop of Reading. Two months later he was obliged to withdraw his acceptance because he was a gay man who had been in a long-term relationship though now celibate and his appointment threatened to split the Anglican Communion. A few days later I was discussing this matter with an Archdeacon and a University Vice-Chancellor. The Vice-Chancellor said 'My children just find the Church of England incredible'. He was not talking about young children nor adolescents but highly intelligent young adults.

The gay issue is not the only one where the church appears not to be listening. The equality of the sexes has been accepted in secular society but not in the church. Women still cannot be appointed bishops. Can it be that God cannot accept fully the ministry of women? Can it be that he wishes us to ignore society's acceptance of human diversity or the concern for the equality of men and women? Can it be that he wishes us to turn our backs on medical and psychological insights into the nature of human sexuality? Of course there is need for theological exploration and the issues are complex and contentious but surely as a church we must be ready to explore the insights which the world offers us, rather than to accept uncritically what St Paul appeared to say to a very different world, and to do so urgently and seriously. Those bells heard by the whole community speak to me of our need to listen to the world.

So on Bell-ringers' Sunday we give thanks to God for the continuity of faith, worship and church life in this village symbolised by the bells. They remind us too of the community and the world in which we try to witness and to which we must also listen – the world of economics and culture and social insights.

1   Address at the Eucharist on Bellringers' Sunday September 2003

Servers' Sunday

Surely the Lord is in this place – and I did not know it. ... This is no other than the house of God and this is the gate of heaven.
Genesis 28.16-17

William Temple, when he was Archbishop of York in the 1930s, was once asked how the world could be saved from chaos and collapse. People wondered whether he would say that a really effective League of Nations would save the world, perhaps the defeat of fascism in Spain, Italy and Germany, or the collapse of Soviet communism. He might even opt for the application of Christian principles to world economic problems. He chose none of those but replied with one word – worship. What an escapist and irrelevant answer, typical of a churchman! But then he explained what he meant by worship.

To worship is to quicken the conscience by the holiness of God; to feed the mind with the truth of God; to purge the imagination with the beauty of God; to open the heart to the love of God; to devote the will to the purpose of God.

Well perhaps worship like that could save the world.

Lay contributors to Anglican worship

We have called today Servers' Sunday in order to recognise and celebrate the contribution to our worship made by the servers, all of whom are robed and sitting in the choir stalls this morning.

But of course servers are not the only lay people who contribute to worship. Many others have a part to play; they include crucifers, acolytes, choristers, organist, lesson readers, intercessors, communion assistants, flower arrangers, sidespersons, coffee makers and the welcome team. I'm sure I must have left some out – of course Readers! In fact there must be few members of the congregation who do not in some way contribute actively to worship. Please regard 'server' as shorthand for all of them. Servers' Sunday provides the opportunity to think not only about the mechanics of worship but about some of the principles which lie behind it and the people who contribute to it.

Simplicity of worship

Let me say first that worship is at the heart of our Christian commitment and that we must never forget that the essence of worship is very simple. There are two sayings of Jesus which summarise this simplicity. 'Where two or three are gathered together in my name, I am there among them'. (Matthew 18.20) 'God is spirit, and those who worship him must worship in spirit and truth'. (John 4.24)

I start there because if we forget that essential simplicity we shall never worship worthily. Liturgy and music, robes and ceremonial, are vehicles which help our worship. They are not ends in themselves. Means are always secondary, the expression of the worship of mind and heart.

Traditions of worship

Let me turn then to the means by which we worship in the Anglican tradi-tion to which we belong at St Peter's. There are of course other traditions of worship. Roman Catholics and Orthodox churches differ in their ways of worship from us, the product of different history and practice over the years. The free churches – Methodist, United Reformed and Baptist for example – place less emphasis on the externals of worship. Their church buildings are simpler and the black robes of their ministers come from the preaching tradition of the Reformation. Their services of Holy Communion have a similar shape to ours but are celebrated more simply, using for example ordinary bread and unfermented grape juice rather than wafers and wine mixed with water. The Society of Friends, often called the Quakers have an even simpler form of worship – they meet in silence and anybody may feel constrained to contribute prayers or thoughts to the assembled company. The externals may be different but the inner reality of worship is the same. But it is about Anglican worship that I speak this morning.

Three characteristics of Anglican worship

We worship through our senses. We approach God through all our senses. We sing hymns, hear Bible readings and a sermon which reach us through speech and hearing. They represent a long tradition of Christian spirituality. But there are other senses through which we worship – touch, sight and even smell. This church has stood here for over 850 years. Its architecture helps us to worship; its carved wood and rich stonework speak of continuity and faithful service. The clergy wear vestments which are graceful, made with skilled craftsmanship, and remind us by their colour of the changing seasons of the Christian year. Choir, servers and acolytes wear robes which exemplify their role in worship.

In all seasons except Advent and Lent flowers chosen and arranged by different people enrich our worship by their scent, colour and arrangement. Gestures contribute to the sense of the presence of God. We bow as we approach the altar; some people genuflect or make the sign of the cross. We may kneel for prayer and to receive Holy Communion. We share the Peace, a Biblical gesture and one which underlines the fellowship we enjoy with each other.

In all these ways and in others we seek to worship with all our senses – with imagination, feelings, and emotions as well as with out minds. At the offertory this morning we shall sing the hymn *Angel voices ever singing,* which includes these words: *'Thou didst ears and hands and voices/ for thy praise design;/ Craftsman's art and music's measure/ for thy pleasure / All combine.*

We worship with Christians through the centuries. Worship takes place in two dimensions. It must be contemporary, expressing the experience of lives lived in the twenty first century but it must also be timeless expressing the unchanging nature of God through 2000 years and more including the experience of the people of the Old Testament expressed in the Psalms.

Servers as well as clergy, Readers and acolytes are wearing a garment called an alb. It looks rather like a nightshirt. It is descended from the white tunic worn by professional people in the Roman Empire. Only after about 400 AD did clerical dress become different from that of ordinary people. The president at the Eucharist wears a chasuble, a garment worn by priests in the catholic tradition when they were celebrating the Eucharist for 1600 years. You will for example find chasubles in the wonderful seventh century mosaics at Ravenna in Italy. The chasuble dropped out of use in England at the Reformation and was not restored until the nineteenth century and only recently have many Anglican churches accepted it.

The offertory procession is a reminder that originally everybody brought their own bread and a flagon of wine and the deacon took it all to the altar at the offertory. Have you wondered why we have a procession with lighted candles before the gospel? In the year 378 St Jerome wrote from Jerusalem 'When the gospel is read lights are kindled as a token of joy and to remind us that the word of God is a lantern to our feet and a light to our path'. So over 1600 years of tradition lies behind the offertory process

I am sometimes asked why the hymn we sing between the lessons and the gospel is called the gradual. Well *gradus* is Latin for step. A solo singer would stand on the altar step to sing a psalm between the epistle and the gospel. That is why we say ' the hymn for the gradual is'…because we are singing a hymn in place of the psalm usual in the medieval church.

So as we worship week by week we are reminded of the company of saints through the ages, in whose company we are meeting. But holding the contemporary and the timeless together is not easy. You will I am sure have heard about the Prayer Book Society whose members feel that the disuse of the Book of Common Prayer in many churches represents an impoverishment of worship just as the disappearance of the timeless prose of the King James Bible was a loss to many. We all have our views about hymns. Worship songs, which mean more to the younger generation, are replacing the classic hymns of the eighteenth century. Keeping both age and youth content is a difficult task.

Through our senses, with all ages and finally:

We worship through everybody's contribution. The word liturgy comes from two Greek words *laos*, which means people and *ergon* which means work, so you could say that liturgy means 'Let the people do the work.' One of the welcome developments in the worship of the Church of England in the last forty years has been the growing contribution of laity. It is partly due to the decline in the number of clergy and the increase in the number of multi-parish benefices but it is also a genuinely theological movement, recognition that we are all, clergy and laity, one people of God. Worship is no longer a clerical monopoly. Readers only came into existence at all in 1866 and it is much more recently that they have taken part in the Eucharist, leading the ministry of the word and sometimes preaching.

As people leave church after the 9.15 service they sometimes say 'I did enjoy the service this morning'. I often wonder what they mean. Was it the hymns – words or music – which helped them? Did the readings and sermon perhaps speak to them? Were the intercessions particularly relevant to their needs or was their reception of Holy Communion particularly significant? Or perhaps it was none of these or all of them, which in some way brought them nearer to God?

My text came from Jacob's vision of the ladder, which rested on the ground but reached to heaven. When he woke Jacob said, 'Surely the Lord is in this place – and I did not know it ... This is no other than the house of God and this is the gate of heaven.' (Genesis 28.16-17) On either side of the great west door of Bath Abbey are two ladders in stone with angels ascending and descending, a reminder that all worship is an interchange between earth and heaven.

COMMEMORATIONS

St Augustine's mission AD 597 [1]

Go therefore and make disciples of all nations, baptising them in the name of the Father and the Son and the Holy Spirit.
Matthew 28.19

Last Sunday 50 pilgrims left Rome to travel through Italy and France following the route taken by St Augustine and his followers 1400 years ago. Today they will land at Pegwell Bay in Kent where Augustine first set foot on English soil.

Yet their journey will be wholly different from St Augustine's. Theirs is more like a package tour; his was an epic adventure, more like a solo voyage round the world or a crossing of Antarctica would be today. They have travelled partly by train and coach; he and the 40 monks in his party accomplished the journey on foot. They are English; assured of a warm welcome from fellow Christians when they arrive; Augustine and his followers didn't speak the language, and feared the hostile reception which they might receive from the fierce, barbarous and pagan Angles of Kent. Their journey took a week; his a year, in part because when he reached France St Augustine took fright and returned to Rome, pleading to be released from such a daunting mission. At the command of Pope Gregory however he set out again and this time completed the journey. So much for comparisons. Let's return to Augustine in 597.

The origin of Augustine's mission

The initiative for the English mission came not from Augustine, who was not really the stuff of which pioneers or even missionaries are made. It came from one of the greatest of the early popes, Gregory the Great. You may remember from school the story of his meeting light skinned, fair haired Englishmen in the slave market in Rome and resolving that one day their fellow countrymen should become not just Angles but angels. His hope of coming to England himself was frustrated by more important duties and it was not until 20 years later, now pope, that Gregory was able to fulfil his ambition to replant the gospel on English soil. It was an ambition not wholly untainted by political considerations. England could and did become strenuously loyal to the pope in Rome and a counterweight to the churches of France and Italy which were substantially under royal control.

Arrival in England

Soon after his arrival in England Augustine met King Ethelbert of Kent, helped by the fact that his queen, Bertha, was already a Christian and that the marriage contract specified that she should be free to practise her faith. She was accompanied to England by a Frankish bishop, Liuthard.

Augustine and his followers were well received. They were allowed to worship freely and to preach the gospel. They were given land on which much later St Augustine's abbey, one of the great abbeys of medieval England, was built. A new museum was built as part of the 1400th anniversary celebrations and was opened recently by the Archbishop of Canterbury. At Christmas 597 it appears that about 10,000 people, led by the king, were baptised into the Christian faith and Kent became at least temporarily a Christian kingdom, even if some of the thegns remained sceptical. Ethelbert's standing in southern England was such that the kingdoms of Essex and East Anglia soon followed.

The nature of Augustine's mission

Let me turn now to the nature of Augustine's mission: first to three things which the mission was not.

It was not the beginning of Christianity in England. At least three centuries before Augustine's arrival there were Christians in England, probably soldiers who brought their faith with them when they were sent to this outpost of the Roman Empire. The first martyrs included St Alban who probably died about 250 AD. There were certainly three English bishops at the Council of Arles in 315.

The work of the Celtic saints in Ireland, Wales, Scotland and the north of England, among them David, Patrick and Columba, was complete before Augustine landed. May 1997 sees a twin commemoration: it marks not only the landing of St Augustine but also the death of St Columba in front of the altar of the abbey he had founded on Iona over 30 years before. In the century after the arrival of Augustine it was the Celtic church which played the larger part in the conversion of England. The abbey of Lindisfarne founded from Iona took the lead in establishing the church in the north of England in the kingdoms of Northumbria and Mercia.

It was not a movement of individual conversion. Those 10,000 people baptised at Christmas 597 did not each experience a personal dedication to Christ, nor go through the Pauline experience of justification by faith. It was a tribal conversion. The faith adopted by the king was the faith of his people, the substitution of one religion for another. The impact of the faith on their lives was gradual rather than dramatic.

It was not a once for all success story. When Augustine died less than ten years after his arrival in England, little further progress had been made. When King Ethelbert died in 616 his successor refused to be baptised and the kingdom of Kent reverted to paganism. Augustine's successor considered fleeing to Gaul. Evangelisation of the remaining Anglo-Saxon territories of southern England had scarcely begun. There were times when it appeared that the English mission inspired by Pope Gregory had failed. It was over a century before England could reasonably be called a Christian country.

The significance of Augustine's mission

It may not have been *the* beginning of Christianity in England but it was *a* beginning, a significant stage in the conversion of England. It was Augustine's main achievement, acting on the instructions of the pope, to begin to create a church organisation which has lasted for 1400 years. The Celtic church may have been strong on spirituality; it was weak on organisation. Its monasteries, largely independent of each other could not provide a long-term framework for church life and expansion. It was the creation of dioceses begun by Augustine on the instructions of pope Gregory and the later creation of territorial parishes, which provided the church in England with the organisational framework which has lasted ever since.

To pope Gregory England was still two Roman provinces, based respectively in London and York. So he instructed Augustine to set up two Christian provinces in London and York, each with twelve dioceses. (The word diocese was not originally an ecclesiastical word at all – simply the name for a Roman province) When Augustine arrived he found London in pagan hands so the southern province was set up at Canterbury and there it has remained ever since. With the conversion of Essex and East Anglia Augustine was able to establish bishoprics at Rochester and London (both date their foundation from 604). What Augustine began Theodore of Tarsus, the greatest archbishop of the next century (668-693), consolidated 80 years later.

Our response to this anniversary

Since this is not just a history lesson let me end with two reflections on the significance of this anniversary and how we might respond to it.

Thanksgiving for our long Christian heritage. It is impossible to assess fully what we owe to our Christian heritage as individuals or as a country. Suffice to say that it has made us the people we are. Every city has its cathedral, often its dominating building. Every town and village has its parish church, often, like our own, by far the largest, oldest and most prominent building for miles around. Cathedrals and churches alike are symbols of the love of God in Christ, which has inspired, cleansed and renewed community and personal life as well as consecrating its most sacred moments – birth, marriage and death. It has influenced for good those apparently indifferent to it as well as those committed to the Christian faith and the Christian church.

Artistic and cultural life owe their inspiration substantially to the gospel – the development of architecture, sculpture, stained glass, painting and music have all been influenced profoundly by the Christian faith. Our laws, our morals, the writing of history and our government are all imbued deeply with Christian ideals. Medicine, education and the care of the poor all arose in this country from Christian inspiration. So our first response to this anniversary must be gratitude to God for what men and women inspired by faith have achieved. We should I believe in the words of the hymn be 'lost in wonder, love and praise'.

We should be grateful too for the twin emphasis of Canterbury and Iona, Augustine and Columba. From the one derived an organisation without which the gospel could not have been spread effectively and consolidated in dioceses and parishes; from the other came a spirituality without which organisation would have been a lifeless shell.

Resolve to safeguard and hand on the heritage. In the days when schools distributed a third of a pint of milk free to all pupils, the late lamented satirical magazine *Punch*, published a cartoon showing school children unloading the milk from crates. The milk lorry had broken down so pupils were throwing the bottles from hand to hand across the playground. Unfortunately the last boy couldn't catch so the bottles, which had passed through a succession of hands, were dropped and the cartoon showed a mess of broken bottles and spilt milk in the gutter.

There is serious danger that our generation could be like that pupil. A tradition passed down through 1400 and more years could be lost because we have failed to hand it on. So our second response to today's celebration must be resolve to do all we can to pass on the Christian heritage into which we have entered. In this parish and deanery we are custodians of a tradition which goes back at least to the year 700AD. It was about then that two men brought up in the minster at Waltham, with the rather odd names of

Boniface and Willibald, set out to preach the gospel to the heathen Germans, just as Augustine had come to pagan Kent some 100 years earlier.

When therefore we worship here each week; when we set out to serve the parish community; when we establish links with Hackney or with the diocese of Calabar in Nigeria; when we develop this building to meet the needs of the next century – we are continuing work which has gone on already for 1400 years or more. Our church life is given depth and significance by the knowledge that we stand in a great and sacred tradition.

1. Address to mark the 1400th anniversary of the landing of St Augustine in Kent in May 1997

᪑

John Wesley [1]

Under 24th May 1738 John Wesley wrote these well-known words in his *Journal*:

'In the evening I went very unwillingly to a society in Aldersgate Street, where one was reading Luther's preface to the Epistle to the Romans. About a quarter before nine, while he was describing the change which God works in the heart through faith in Christ, I felt my heart strangely warmed. I felt I did trust in Christ, Christ alone for salvation; and an assurance was given me, that he had taken away my sins and saved me from the law of sin and death...'

Methodists celebrate the 24th May as Wesley Day, the anniversary of John Wesley's conversion. But it was not really a conversion. Wesley had been deeply serious about his faith since his days at Oxford in the early 1720s; he was ordained deacon in 1725 and priest in 1728 and served for a time as his father's curate. After his father's death in 1735 he was briefly a missionary, though not a very successful one, in the newly founded American colony of Georgia. If 24th May 1738 was not Wesley's conversion it marked an equally momentous landmark in his life: the beginning of his evangelical ministry, which was to last for over 50 years until his death in 1791 and to have a decisive effect on the church and the country.

John Wesley was the most influential churchman in the English-speaking world between Richard Hooker in the seventeenth century and John Henry Newman in the nineteenth century. This year is the 300th anniversary of his birth in June 1703 and it is being celebrated not only by Methodists worldwide but also by the church universal.

John Wesley the man

John Wesley was born at Epworth Rectory in Lincolnshire, the 13th or 14th child (nobody seems quite sure which) and second surviving son of Samuel and Susannah. He was educated at Charterhouse, then in the city of London, and at Christ Church Oxford and in 1726 became a Fellow of Lincoln College.

Following his 'heart warming' experience in 1738 he began to travel the country in his own words 'to spread scriptural holiness throughout the land'. He travelled on horseback until extreme old age forced him to take to coach travel. He moved in the early years in a triangle between London, Newcastle-on-Tyne and Bristol. But this was not the limit of his travels. By the end of the 1740s he had visited Cornwall, the Midlands, Ireland and the north of Scotland and by the end of his life there was scarcely a town in the country where he had not at some time preached. He is reckoned to have travelled about 250,000 miles on land and sea and to have preached some 40,000 sermons. He displayed throughout his life vigour and restless activity, which would have put even Mrs Thatcher in the shade. He rose between 4 and 5 am, and preached in the open air for the last time when he was 87.

He was short – about 5 feet 3inches tall – and slight of build weighing just over 8 stone, neat in appearance, with a restrained manner. Often denied the use of the parish church he preached in the open air, at first reluctantly. He wrote in his Journal for 31st May 1739:

> 'I could scarce reconcile myself at first to this strange way of preaching in the fields, of which [Mr Whitfield] set me an example on Sunday; having been all my life so tenacious of every point relating to decency and order, that I should have thought the saving of souls almost a sin, if it had not been done in a church.'

Two days later he wrote 'At four in the afternoon, I submitted to be more vile, and proclaimed in the highways the glad tidings of salvation, speaking from a little eminence in a ground adjoining to the city, to about 3000 people'. The city was Bristol. He was soon attracting huge crowds and often a good deal of hostility.

Wesley was not however an eighteenth century Billy Graham. He was steeped in Anglican theology, a disciple of William Law, as well as Roman Catholic writers. He read voraciously often on horseback. He was a churchman with a far higher sacramental doctrine than was usual in the eighteenth century Church of England. He urged 'continual communion', regarded the Lord's Supper as a 'converting ordinance' and a vital means of grace. He both received and celebrated communion frequently throughout his life and urged his followers to do the same.

Some Methodists in nineteenth and twentieth centuries idolised Wesley. He was of course like all of us a fallible mortal. He shared the eighteenth century belief in witchcraft and would open his Bible at random and expect to receive guidance. He was naturally authoritarian, disciplined to the point of obsession, and never idle. His dealings with women were a blind spot. He married in 1751, already in his 40s, Mary Vazeille, the widow of a city banker and mother of four children. It was a disastrous mistake. They soon separated perhaps because Wesley announced that he intended to travel not one mile less nor preach one less sermon as a consequence of being a married man!

Wesley and the Church of England

From the beginning Wesley saw his mission as the spiritual renewal of a lethargic Church of England and he had no intention of creating a new denomination. 'I live and die in the Church of England', he said. He taught nothing contrary to the Prayer Book, the Thirty Nine Articles and the Homilies of the Church of England. Right up to the time of his death he never formally separated nor had he been excluded from the Church of England. He would not allow Methodist services to compete with those of the parish church so they often took place at 5 o'clock in the morning.

Why then did Wesley's followers separate from the Church of England and create a new denomination so soon after his death? From the beginning Wesley's peripatetic ministry was at odds with the parish system of the established church. When he famously said 'The world is my parish' he did not mean that he felt called to work in the overseas church. Instead he meant quite simply that his calling could not be contained within the limits of any one parish where his preaching would be constrained by episcopal licence. He was a born organiser and almost from the beginning made provision for his followers to continue to meet when he was no longer with them and thus created structures which were not compatible with Anglican discipline. He formed his followers into societies with rules to ensure that 'they walked worthy of the gospel', into smaller groups called classes and the even more intimate 'bands' where spiritual life was nurtured. The societies were gathered into 'circuits' in which in due course Wesley's preachers would be stationed. (Societies, classes, circuits and 'stations' are still part of the distinctive vocabulary of Methodism). From 1744 he held an annual conference of his preachers, which is the ancestor of the Methodist Conference of the present day.

From 1739 Wesley made use of what came to be called local preachers. These were men – no women were formally appointed by the Wesleyan Methodist church until 1918 – who preached while continuing in their ordinary job. (Itinerant preachers were full time, liable to be moved to a new place frequently and were the forerunners of the Methodist ministry.) It is reckoned that even today seven out of every ten Methodist services are taken by local preachers. Wesley used lay people as class leaders as well as local preachers at a time when the Church of England would not countenance lay spiritual leaders. There were no Readers in the Church of England until 1866 and even then their role was a very limited one.

Gradually it became clear that Wesley had created an organisation which was not compatible with the Church of England as it then was. By the time he died there were 72,000 Methodists in Great Britain and 43,000 in USA. Fifty years later that number had multiplied tenfold. Many of Wesley's followers were from the new towns, which developed as a result of the Industrial Revolution, and from the social class least likely to be drawn to the parish churches as they were. The new wine could not be contained in the old wine skins and long before Wesley's death a parting of the ways looked likely.

There was however one issue which made separation inevitable. In 1784 John Wesley ordained Thomas Coke for service in USA and later for work in the British Isles. In the Church of England only a bishop can ordain. Wesley had come to believe that in the New Testament there was no distinction between presbyter and bishop and he had some Anglican opinion on his side. It was however an act of which Charles Wesley disapproved and which the Church of England could not overlook.

The hymns of Methodism

Let me finally say something about the hymns of the Wesleys. Most of them were of course by Charles Wesley. John wrote a small number and translated more from German. Hymns were a crucial part of the Methodist enterprise. Hymns were illegal in the worship of the Church of England until the early nineteenth century. Prayer Book services were dreary and music was confined to metrical versions of the Psalms. Much of the appeal of Methodist services lay in their use of hymns. Charles Wesley was by far the most prolific hymn writer of all time composing as many as 6,500 hymns. In 1779 John Wesley produced one of the earliest hymnbooks. It has a title which resonates: *Hymns for the use of the people called Methodists* and Wesley described it 'a little body of experimental and practical divinity'. It was biblical and doctrinal; the hymns were expressed in memorable verse. And of course they were not meant just to sing in services. They enriched the spiritual life of people as they went about their daily work. They were sung to tunes which were lively and singable. Sadly we have but a pitifully small selection in current Anglican hymnbooks. I hope that in our adoption of what we now sometimes call 'worship songs' we shall never lose the great Wesley hymns – *O for a thousand tongues, Love divine all loves excelling, O thou who camest from above, Christ whose glory fills the skies, Hark the herald angels sing* for example.

The Church of England and the Methodist Church in the twenty first century

The separation of the followers of John Wesley from the Church of England in the late eighteenth century was probably inevitable. Their continuing separation two centuries later was not. For 14 years from 1955 to 1969 there were what were called Conversations between the two churches with a view to reunion. On 8th July 1969 I sat in the gallery of the Methodist Conference meeting that year in Birmingham and listened to the debate on the final report of the Conversations. The Conference voted for unity with the Church of England with a 78% majority. We waited in tense silence for the result of the vote of the Church of England Convocations meeting in London. The scheme for union was rejected by the Church of England with a vote of 69% in favour. Why the necessary majority had been fixed at 75% it is impossible to say. (It is hard to imagine anything on which 75% of the Church of England would agree!) It was in my view and that of many Anglicans including Archbishop Michael Ramsey, one of the saddest days in the history of the church in this country in the twentieth century. I am glad we have begun to talk again though hesitantly in the light of the sad experience of the twentieth century.

But finally a note of gratitude. The celebration of the 300th anniversary of the birth of John Wesley is an opportunity to thank God for his life and ministry. The evangelical revival of the eighteenth century was not the work of Wesley alone nor was it confined to the British Isles but John Wesley was the towering figure and without him the church of the late eighteenth and early nineteenth century would have been the poorer. We are all the beneficiaries of his life and ministry. Thanks be to God.

1 Address to mark the 300th anniversary of the birth of John Wesley on 17th June 1703.

The Millennium [1]

See, now is the acceptable time; see, now is the day of salvation!
2 Corinthians 6.2b

We owe the millennium to a Greek-speaking monk from Southern Russia named Dionysius Exiguus, who lived in the first half of the sixth century. If you want to cut him down to size, translate his name into English and he becomes Dennis the Short. We can imagine his fellow monks calling Shortie – or something even ruder – round the cloisters. He was asked by the pope to come up with a way of calculating the date of Easter and he ended up inventing AD and BC. He counted the years back to the conception of Jesus on 25th March in the Year One. Subsequent years were Years of our Lord, in Latin 'Anni Domini'. He was probably about four years out in his calculations – many people think Jesus was born in 4 BC – but the remarkable thing is, not that he made a mistake, but that he was so close. Centuries elapsed before the Christian era was widely accepted. In England it was popularised by another monk the Venerable Bede, a century and a half after the time of Dennis the Short.

The Christian view of time

But Dennis had stumbled on something of profound significance. On this last but one Sunday not just of the year, or even the century but of a millennium of the Christian era, something which will not occur again for 40 generations, I want to speak about the Christian view of time. It is also a theme which is appropriate for Advent.

The dating of our history from the birth of Jesus reminds us that every event takes place for a Christian in a Year of our Lord. Increasingly in schools and elsewhere the phrase Common Era (CE) is replacing Anno Domini (AD), in deference to our multi-faith society, but for Christians the Year of our Lord remains not only a conventional way of dating but a constant reminder of our view of history. Our year is a celebration of the Year of our Lord, the recital of events which took place 2000 years ago but which are still of vital significance for us and against which all secular events are to be judged.

There are two ideas tied together in our word time – time as duration and time as purpose. We use time mostly in the first sense to express a sequence of events which follow each other.

In the Bible this is reversed; time is chiefly related to purpose, to the significance of events and only secondarily to the passing of the years.

Two words for time

This contrast between time as duration and time as purpose is underlined in Greek by the use of two different words for time – *chronos* and *kairos*. *Chromos* is time measured by the clock and the calendar, time reckoned in days, months and years; the word which passes into English in chronology, chronometer, chronicle and chronic – when an illness lasts a long time. In Matthew chapter 2 verse 7 for example 'The time the star appeared' is *chronos*.

The Greek word *kairos* has no English equivalent. It is the word used in Greek when we say 'I chose the right time to tell her'; 'The time was ripe'; 'It was the opportune moment'. It is a word which means time plus opportunity, time as a crossroads, time when circumstances are favourable, when people are in the right place, when events can be moulded. It is this word *kairos* which is characteristic of the New Testament. Time is not just one thing after another; it is time with a purpose, time for decision, time as crisis. Above all the coming of Jesus is a *kairos* – a time of fulfilment, a time of opportunity when delay would be fatal. From the very beginning of his ministry Jesus proclaimed the coming of the Kingdom of God as a *kairos*.

Time in the New Testament

No passage in the New Testament illustrates this better than that vivid parable of the two kinds of bridesmaids at the wedding feast in Matthew 25 with its concluding warning ' Keep awake for you know neither the day nor the hour' (verse 13). The great Advent hymn *Sleepers, Awake*, which we shall sing in a few minutes to J.S.Bach's setting of Philip Nicolai's superb and moving tune, is based in part on that passage: *Come forth ye virgins wise; the Bridegroom comes, arise; Each lamp be bright with ready light, to grace the marriage feast tonight'*.

When Jesus sends his disciples to prepare the last Passover which he is to share with them he tells them to say 'The teacher says my time is near (*kairos*)'(Matthew 26.18). In the first chapter of Acts after the Resurrection the disciples want to know 'Is this the time when you will restore the kingdom to Israel' Jesus replies 'It is not for you to know the times' (vv.6-7). Again the word is *kairos*.

But the *kairos*, the time of opportunity, doesn't end with the death and resurrection of Jesus. The early church lived its life with the same sense that the time of decision was imminent. There was no time for delay. The New Testament letters are full of the need for urgency and frequently use the word *kairos* to convey it. For example Paul writes to the Romans: 'You know what time it is (*kairon*), how it is the moment for you to wake out of sleep ... the night is far gone, the day is near.' (13.11) The writer of the letter to the Ephesians says: 'Redeem the time.'(*kairon*)(5.16) or as New English Bible translates it 'Use the present opportunity to the full'. And finally the text with which I began this morning from the Second Letter to the Corinthians:' Now is the acceptable time (*kairos)*, now is the day of salvation'.(6.2)

Failure to discern the kairoi

Yet all too often it seems we take exactly the opposite view of time from the one we find in the New Testament. We use the phrase 'In God's good time', to mean, 'Not now', ' Not yet', 'Not while I'm in charge', or even 'Over my dead body'. We behave as though there is, as we say 'All the time in the world', so that our instinctive inertia, our vested interests, are not disturbed. We fail too often to discern the *kairoi*.

Let me apply what I believe the New Testament is saying about time as opportunity, to the events of our time. I want to give you three examples of where is seems to me there was a failure to discern a *kairos*.

First: the twentieth century in Britain has been dominated by the tragedy of Ireland. Only now in 1999 is there the beginning of a solution and even today it is precarious. Just over a century ago a great Christian statesman, William Ewart Gladstone, believed that Home Rule for the whole of Ireland was the solution to a problem already longstanding and intractable. He felt this so strongly that after failing to achieve it in 1886, he became Prime Minister for the fourth time in 1893 at the age of 83. He failed through defeat in the House of Lords. I believe the Irish problem might have been solved in the 1890s before attitudes on both sides hardened irrevocably. It was a *kairos*, a moment of opportunity. Failure to discern it is writ large over the history of the twentieth century.

Second: in 1953 the minister of Wesley church in Cambridge announced to his congregation one Sunday morning that he would be leaving to serve in Rhodesia, now Zimbabwe. He had only been minister for a very short time and was a very effective minister of a church with a large university congregation. He believed however that Southern Africa was about to face its moment of crisis and he felt called to leave Cambridge and minister there. He did so. Years later he wrote ' I found on the main issue I was right. Rhodesia [now Zimbabwe] did face its moment of crisis between 1955 and 1960. I could give you chapter and verse to prove that Christians were confronted with the truth of the hour.' They were strangely unseeing – the *kairos* was not discerned. And the consequences of that failure too have been evident ever since.

Third: in 1964 the British Council of Churches, as it then was, called on its member churches to unite, it dared to hope by Easter 1980. We had been talking about unity since at least 1920; you might think 60 years would be enough even for the church. But Easter 1980 came and went and we are still divided. We failed to discern the *kairos*. Our rivalries and vested interests, our institutional survival took precedence over what we still believe in theory but not in practice to be the will of God, that we should be united. And the decline of the free churches since then has been even more spectacular than that of the Church of England and the Roman Catholic church.

The challenge of the Millennium

I have illustrated the Christian view of time from three major issues of this century- Ireland, Southern Africa and Church unity. But the same principles apply to the decisions with which we are confronted. It is time to mend a family rift, time to face a decision we have postponed, time to accept a new challenge or a new job: God's time, his *kairos* confronts us. We are called to heed the parable of the bridesmaids at the wedding feast and the words of St Paul, 'Now is the acceptable time, now is the day of salvation'. The Christian message for the millennium is, I believe, that we should take seriously the urgency of the tasks we are set in our day and in the new century and the new millennium.

I want to close with an illustration and a quotation.

Before the war there was a shop in the Strand, near Charing Cross station which sold cheap souvenirs for visitors to London. One day a notice appeared outside which read, ' Closing sale', so visitors knew that this was their last opportunity, it was no use coming back next week, the sale would be over, the shop closed and the chance gone for ever. But lo and behold six months later there was another notice which said 'Positively the last few days. Great closing sale'. Once more no doubt the unsuspecting visitor rushed to buy. Then came the Blitz on London, the area was flattened and the shop was no more. But a day or so later among the debris a notice appeared: 'Positively the last few days. Great salvage sale'. That parable contains the paradox of the Christian view of time: the moment of decision is always now, yet God always gives us another opportunity.

And the quotation. It is from Professor Herbert Butterfield, a Christian historian whose lectures I went to at Cambridge. In his book *Christianity and History* he wrote 'The purpose of life is not in the far future nor, as we so often imagine, round the next corner but the whole of it is here and now as fully as it will ever be on this planet'. [2]

'Now is the acceptable time, now is the day of salvation.'

1 Sermon preached on the Fourth Sunday of Advent, 19th December 1999
2 Herbert Butterfield *Christianity and History* G.Bell 1950 p.66

Biblical References

References are to the New Revised Standard Version (NRSV) except where otherwise indicated in the text.

Genesis	1.22	107		Ecclesiastes	1-12	100-104
	1.31	73			3.7	143
	2.7, 18	103				
	11.1-9	40,43		Isaiah	7.14	109
	19.24-26	90			45.15	113
	25-33	95			60.1-6	21,22
	28.16-17	151,155				
	29.15-30	93		Ezekiel	34, 7-16	97, 99
	30.31-43	93				
	32.13-31	92		Amos	7.14-15	98
Exodus	13	25		Zechariah	14.20	148
	16.13-26	138				
	22.25	92		Matthew	1.1-25	107-110
	39.25	148			2.1-12	21
					2.7	167
Leviticus	12	25			5.15	104
	25.35,38	92			6.10	73
					10.3	111
Deuteronomy	6.4-5	46			14.13-22	137
	23.19-20	92			15.32-39	137
					18.20	152
Joshua	9.21,27	92			19.14-15	86
					20.14	118
Judges	5.26	90			24.1-51	13
					25.13, 18	167
1 Samuel	1.19-28	24			28.19	45,157
	15.33	90			28.29	85
	17.33-35	99				
				Mark	2.1-12	76-77
2 Kings	2.23-25	90			3.18	111
	4.42-44	138			4.34	104
					6.32-45	137
Job	23.3	113			8.1-10	137
					12.28-31	82
Psalms	8.4-5	57			13.1-37	13
	22.1	113				
	23	97		Luke	1.52-53	115
	72.10-11	21			2.22-40	24
	150. 3-5	148			2.32-39	26
					6.15	111,116
Proverbs	13.24	92			7.2-10	26
					9.10-17	137
					14.1-24	114-117
					15.6	99

Book	Ref	Page		Book	Ref	Page
Luke	15.11-32	78		Romans	5.1-2	60,63,127
	15.22-24	62			7.18,24	127
	18.9-14	63			8.1-2	127
	21.5-36	13			8.21	60
	24.13-35	30,32-36			8.38-39	127
	24.39,42	30			10.9	55
	24.50-52	36-39			12.1-2	27,127
					12.1-5	24
John	1.1	133			13.10	80,84
	1.14	20,89			13.11	13,168
	1.16-17	133,135			13.14	125
	2.1-11	133-36,140				
	3.16	73,133		1 Corinthians	2.1-2	122
	4.24	152			8.6	55
	4.46-54	140			11.23-26	138
	5.2-9	140			12.2	54
	5.39-40	89			13.1-13	31,83
	6.1-14	136-39			15.8	126
	6.4-13	140				
	9.1-7	140		2 Corinthians	5.17,19	78,126
	10.7-16	97			6.2	166,168,170
	11.1-44	139-142			8.9	83
	11.16	111			13.14	45
	11.25	139				
	14.2,6	133		Ephesians	1-6	128-132
	14.5-6	111,133			2.18	44
	20.2	30			3.1-12	21,22
	20.15,19,27	30			5.16	168
	20.17	38			5.25	64
	20.29	29,111				
	21.15-17	99		Philippians	2. 5-11	53-54,83
Acts	1.6-7	167		Colossians	3.1	142
	1.9	37				
	1.13	112		1 Timothy	2.11-15	91
	2.1-21	40-44			3.14-21	55
	2.41	85				
	8.36-38	85		Hebrews	7.24	67
	8.37	55			13.8	36,38
	9.18	85				
	13.16-41	121		1 Peter	1.8	114
	16.15,33	86			2.9-10	64,67
	17.22-31	121-24			5.1-4	97,99
Romans	1.1,7	48		1 John	4.10	80,84
	1.17	61				
	3.23	127		2 John	vv.7-8	17,19

The Reverend Whitfield Foy MC 1916–1990 [1]

Whitfield Foy was born on 1st November 1916 in the mining village of New Delaval, Blyth, Northumberland, of Wesleyan Methodist parents, the youngest of six children. His father was an under-manager at the local pit. He went to Blyth Grammar School where he became a football player of distinction and, before his school days were over, a local preacher. It was here too that he met Rachel whom he was to marry in 1943.

He was accepted as a candidate for the Methodist ministry and was sent for training to Headingley College, Leeds in 1937 remaining there for four years and taking a Leeds university BA degree and, after leaving college, a London BD degree. He spent the next two years as a probationary minister in Leeds, was ordained in 1943 and volunteered for army chaplaincy. He was posted to the 13th Battalion, the Parachute Regiment, part of the famed 6th Airborne Division. He parachuted into Normandy on the night before D Day landing 15 miles from the intended rendezvous point and again into Germany in April 1945 for the crossing of the Rhine.

He was an outstanding padre respected by officers and men alike and by the non-combatants attached to the unit as medical orderlies. He was awarded the Military Cross during the Ardennes campaign in January 1945. Searching for casualties he drove an ambulance-jeep within point blank range of a German tank. The astonished tank commander held his fire and emerged from his turret shouting 'You may collect your wounded this time but don't come back again!'

When the war in Europe was over he served in the Far East returning to civilian life in 1946. In 1947 he was sent as minister to the famous Brunswick Church, Leeds where before the war Leslie Weatherhead and W.E.Sangster had preached to packed congregations. It was a daunting assignment for a man only 30 years of age. The congregation was still substantial and used to distinguished preachers. The church was also the headquarters of the University Methodist Society then expanding with the return of men from the war.

After five years in Leeds he came in 1952, a year earlier than he had expected, to Wesley Church Cambridge, then at its zenith. There was a packed morning congregation numbering up to 500, the church often full during the university term, as well as a strong congregation mostly of townspeople at night. The University Methodist Society had over 400 members. He was a preacher of quite outstanding gifts in the last era when people listened to sermons and preaching was still central to the ministry of the free churches.

His sermons were biblical but he was not an expository preacher. He rarely announced a text maintaining that much un-biblical preaching was concealed by a text. On Monday he would read the lessons for the following Sunday. Using commentary and conversation, headline and editorial, film and radio, events ecclesial and worldly, anecdote and encounter, he brought each to bear on the lessons, and the lessons on them. By Saturday he was ready to shape the sermon, reducing it to brief notes on a card, which alone accompanied him into the pulpit. The theme would be announced and its application to personal, social and public life expounded and illustrated. He was an enemy of platitude and cliché. If ever there was a servant of the Word it was Whit Foy. The opening of the sermon was calculated to compel attention usually with some memorable anecdote. Consider this opening to a sermon for All Saints tide.

One of my first explorations into sin took place when, then a small boy, I put a halfpenny on the counter of the village shop, and asked for one of *those*, – for my dad, please'. *Those* were well known cigarettes which retailed at five for two pence. And I can remember the benign appearance of the shopkeeper who knew my father well, and knew perfectly well that he smoked a pipe. He looked at me and said with a quiet but feigned sadness, 'I'm sorry son, they don't come in ones'. So I settled for marshmallows.

As a consequence of that illustration I shall always remember that saints 'don't come in ones', and that the term for saint in the New Testament is plural and means 'all God's people'.

Those who heard him preach will never forget the experience. He was under divine compulsion. He was short of stature, his voice was not strong but had an attractive Northumberland lilt; in the pulpit he compelled attention. I count it one of the seminal experiences of my life to have sat regularly under his preaching during my university career. His preaching, pastoral care and friendship sustained and encouraged generations of students. In 1955 no less than nine men (women could not then be ordained in the Methodist church) from Cambridge were candidates for the Methodist ministry; several of them were to become the leaders of the church in the rest of the twentieth century.

He became increasingly concerned about the hold which fundamentalism had on many undergraduates. When Billy Graham came to Harringey in 1954 I recall his announcing that next Sunday he would preach on 'The Gospel of Billy Graham', a sermon in which he tellingly compared the simplicity of the gospel expounded by Jesus with the razzmatazz associated with the Billy Graham mission.

In January 1954 he told a shocked congregation that he would be leaving Wesley Church in August 1955, after only three years, to work under the Methodist Missionary Society in what was then Southern Rhodesia. Cambridge he had concluded was something of an ivory tower. The future lay in Africa. He became minister of the Central (English) Church on Third Street, Salisbury. Here he attempted to encourage African/European integration and to hasten African progress to political power. With Nathan Shamuyarira, later minister in the Zimbabwe government and Terence Ranger, warden of the University Halls of Residence and later Professor of African Studies at Oxford, he worked through the Christian Action Group to draw attention to racial injustice. But sadly it was too much for many members of his church and they narrowly failed to invite him for a further period when his first term came to an end in 1960. He preached a final sermon from Isaiah chapter 6 verse 1. '*I saw the Lord sitting on a throne, high and lifted up*'. On the strength of his ministry in Rhodesia he must rank as one of the foremost yet unsung Christian prophets of the twentieth century.

He came back to England hoping to return to Africa, to follow Colin Morris as minister of Chingola Free Church on the Copperbelt. Sadly ill health prevented this and he spent the remaining years of his ministry in England briefly at Golders Green and for five years in York. In 1967 he returned to Wesley Church, Cambridge and a further distinguished preaching ministry ensued. However he developed angina and towards the end was obliged to preach sitting down. He retired from active ministry in 1971 at the early age of 54 but remained living in Cambridge and after a heart bypass operation at Papworth hospital in August 1978 was able to preach regularly and take pastoral responsibility for the village church at Toft on the outskirts of Cambridge.

He published no book of sermons but in his last year as minister of Wesley Church he agreed to his sermons being tape recorded and then transcribed. The result was a modest spiral bound book of 22 sermons which he entitled *Shots fired in retreat,* of which I possess a pirated copy. The title reflected his impending retirement but as he says in his Preface 'in retreat, is a phrase not entirely inapplicable to the church as a whole in the West', a sombre thought but one consonant with the realism of this man of faith.

1. I have drawn for this brief memoir on the address given at the Thanksgiving service for Whitfield Foy at Wesley Church, Cambridge in March 1990 and on the obituary notice in *The Methodist Recorder,* both by the Revd Brian Duckworth, one of the men who entered the Methodist ministry from Cambridge in 1955. Sadly he died in 2003.